"Rooted in an unshakable commitment to equity, compassion, and interdependence, Bloomberg and Pitchford have further developed their Leading Impact Teams framework to guide school communities in redefining how the learning process can empower students and teachers in such a way that each is elevated by it. This book speaks seamlessly across the worlds of scholarship and implementation, and it provides a straightforward path to engage existing structures in schools to take deeper steps toward "learning" as a partnership between educators, students, families, and the wider community. Ultimately, Impact Teams helps us practically imagine how schools become spaces of leadership, where the challenges of an increasingly dynamic world are able to be contemplated by those students who will quickly inherit the responsibility to shoulder it."

**—Sam Jordan**
Grants Director, Alaska Council of School Administrators,
Palmer, Alaska

"This book champions the transformative power of collaboration. It provides practical methods, actionable insights, reflective questions, and exemplars to guide and empower educators. These methods have all been tried and tested by the authors and the numerous districts and schools they have worked with. The book reflects a deep commitment to equity, a keen focus on using evidence and inquiry to inform practice, and a commitment to ensuring that learners are active participants in the learning process. These, together, are fundamental building blocks to ensure that every learner receives the education they deserve. Leading Impact Teams 2.0 is an essential guide for those passionate about making a difference."

**—Anna Sullivan**
Chief Executive, Evaluation Associates Ltd.,
Newmarket, New Zealand

"The revised edition of Bloomberg and Pitchford's Leading Impact Teams has strengthened and clarified a book that has already become one of the most implemented professional development sources for instructional teams around the world. The focus of moving teams from PLCs to Impact Teams is the mission of this book through the strategy of teacher collective *efficacy. This new edition adds important dimensions of impact and efficacy through a focus on equity, asset-based pedagogies, and culturally responsive instruction. Instructional teams will continue to learn how to maximize collective efficacy through learning cultures, feedback, and formative mindsets, but with an increased focus on diverse populations that stand to benefit from this important instructional model."*

**—Barry J. Graff, EdD**
Brigham Young University–Public School Partnership,
Provo, Utah

*"I'm pleased that Bloomberg and Pitchford courageously call out the inherent inequities in our educational system that have long existed and have resulted in disparate experiences and outcomes for a majority of black and brown children causing generational harm. Impact Teams 2.0 masterfully identifies "what, why, and how" to create efficacious teams of learners focused on the learning process, noting that students, teachers, and family are all learners and an important part of this work. Equity is clearly defined, and a culturally responsive lens is intentionally integrated in every key aspect of the design and implementation of the Impact Team Model. This book is a must-read for district leaders, principals, and teachers ready to take their PLC and leadership teams to the next level."*

**—Dr. Michele Bowers**
superintendent emeritus, founder of Vital Educational
Leadership Consulting, and chair of the National Coalition on
Educational Equity, Henderson, Nevada

*"Leading Impact Teams 2.0 offers busy educators a practical, thoughtful, and powerful resource. The updated version is both significant and timely in supporting educators to deeply reflect on equity and harness the transformative power of relationships. No starting point or journey is the same, but the combination of the framework, the reflective questions, and examples in this book means no matter where you start, you can find your way."*

**—Sarah Philip**
educational psychologist and coach, Haddington
East Lothian, Scotland

"In Leading Impact Teams, Paul and Barb do something that every school leader, teacher leader, and collaborative team needs from a book: they make clear, succinct connections between theory, research, and practice. In a time where there are so many "actions" that teams can take to meet the diverse and ever-changing needs of the learners in their schools, it's refreshing to see a resource that gives teams practical strategies to focus on the IMPACT of their collaborative actions where it matters the most—in the classroom with students and educators. With entry points for any team, regardless of where they are on their collaborative learning trajectory, Leading Impact Teams is a must-read!"

**—Cale Birk**
former head of innovation, school principal, observable impact imagineer, and coauthor of *Navigating Leadership Drift: Observable Impact on Rigorous Learning* (2023, with Michael McDowell) and *PLC 2.0: Collaborating for Observable Impact in Today's Schools* (2019, with Garth Larson), Kamloops, BC, Canada

"This book had me hooked in the introduction, where Bloomberg and Pitchford remind us: "Our current educational system was not created to ensure that all students achieve at high levels. Our system has been created to focus on competition, deficits, assimilation, and hierarchy." They make the case of the need to address this inequity in a systemic way to ensure all students learn at high levels—an oft-desired goal of all schools! More importantly, as a grandfather of six, I hope my colleagues in this profession do take up the Impact Team challenge and build the type of school where each one of my grandkids (and all their peers) not only succeeds by traditional measures but thrives in the more inclusive world they will enter."

**—Tom Hierck**
best-selling author and consultant, Gibsons, BC, Canada

"Bloomberg and Pitchford's Leading Impact Teams 2.0 is exceptional! This is well written and easy to digest. It is an absolute must-read for teacher teams and educational leaders who are looking to level up their teamwork—especially those who are addressing equity gaps! My favorite *part of each chapter was the Team and Equity Reflection questions. I will be recommending this book to my entire personal learning network!"*

**—Mari Braithwaite**
professional learning and curriculum director, Alpine School District, Utah

*"As a district, our principals began the journey of using the Impact Team approach to empower teachers to focus on their pedagogical skills, curriculum, and student progress. Moving the emphasis to teacher teams and having the book as a guide ensured that the professional learning teams were aligned, organized, and focused. The step-by-step facilitation guide was a game changer for our schools and district. Having all of our 70 schools, from PreK–12, speaking the same common language allows us to seamlessly share best practices, visit each other's schools, and provide strategic and clear feedback that leads to increased student learning."*

**—Vincenza Gallassio**
former superintendent, New York City District 31

*"Reading this book was akin to unpacking a suitcase of the highest-quality garments. I felt invited to "try on" approaches to learning that are growth-fostering and life-affirming, which stand in sharp contrast to the drill-and-kill emphasis of the last 40 years in American education. The book's unrelenting focus on the assets of learners and its profound respect for every stakeholder in the community are much-needed antidotes to the century-long deficit orientation that sees young people as problems to be solved. Kudos to the authors and their collaborators across the country for reminding us of the importance of relational trust among educators and that collective efficacy is the most reliable energy source for more engaged student learning."*

**—Jane Feinberg**
executive director, Power of Place Learning Communities, Belmont, Massachusetts

*"Impact Teams 2.0 takes collective efficacy to the next level. The authors*

*provide you with this updated step-by-step guide to superpower your team so you can make a positive impact on student learning through equitable systems, collaborative inquiry, and effective team actions. Impact Teams helps you make a difference!"*

**—Jennifer Wildman, EdD**
former superintendent, Bend, Oregon

*"Bloomberg and Pitchford wrote a one-stop-shop book for every administrator and teacher leader who wants to lift and build their PLCs and Impact Teams to the next level by empowering all students. This inspirational read includes all crucial parts to nurture school systems by providing opportunity, accessibility, and advancement for all students. It's a breath of fresh air to learn new approaches based on students, for students, and without the political content. Paul and Barb cunningly designed this book to build efficacy in cultivating a school culture of learners and incorporating all stakeholders. This teacher-friendly book is straight to the point, easy to implement, and packed with opportunities to run PLCs that impact all students."*

**—Delia Duncan**
central office reading support teacher, San Diego Unified
School District, California

*"Bloomberg and Pitchford have strengthened an already powerful tool in the second edition of Leading Impact Teams, which will benefit any teacher, teacher leader, school leader, or even district leader. With an emphasis on efficacy, this new edition not only explains what efficacy means at all levels of the school system, but it shows you how to recognize and strengthen self-efficacy, student efficacy, and collective teacher efficacy—the most impactful element of a school system. This, mixed with the new tools around how to develop agency, allows Barb and Paul to take you and your team along a journey toward success in any school system."*

**—Cheryle Lerch**
district administrator, Fort Bend ISD, Sugar Land, Texas

"While a great deal of resources around collaboration and professional learning communities exists, Impact Teams 2.0 stands out as a methodology that has evolved to have a greater impact, based on the feedback of students, teachers, and leaders. In other words, it's a process crafted from research and made tried and true by educators. If you wish to improve collaboration that is focused on efficacy and honors equity, it's a must-read!"

**—Kara Vandas**

consultant and best-selling coauthor, *Clarity for Learning: Five Essential Practices That Empower Students and Teachers* (2018, with John Almarode), Castle Rock, Colorado

"In this next iteration of Impact Teams, Paul and Barb have expertly drawn on their personal experience and most up-to-date research to create a detailed guide for leaders and teachers interested in empowering teams, acutely focused on improving outcomes for all learners. They make the case for genuine and purposeful collaborative inquiry, grounded in evidence and relational trust with students and families at its core. They present a thought-provoking narrative around social network theory and how it is integral to the infrastructure of effective teams. If you are ready to begin strengthening teacher teams for impact, then this book equips you with the research, framework, and tools to empower your teams and enable the success of all learners."

**—Laura McWhinnie**

director of education, Embrace Multi Academy Trust, Leicestershire, England, and former director of Visible Learning Plus UK, Birmingham, England

"While common planning time is a ubiquitous structure in our schools, team meetings don't always deliver on their promise of sustained professional learning that has an impact on student achievement and well-being. Authors Bloomberg and Pitchford have written a clear and compelling guide to leading teacher teams that are squarely focused on nurturing student agency. Such high-functioning teams harness the power of collective *efficacy to create conditions in which every student can ultimately take charge of their own learning. The authors not only have an in-depth understanding of teaching and learning but approach their endeavor with humility and a sincere respect for the work of teachers. With an explicit focus on advancing culturally responsive and sustaining practice, Leading Impact Teams makes a significant contribution to the PLC literature."*

**—Dan Alpert**
program director and publisher, Corwin Press,
Palm Springs, California

*"Leading Impact Teams 2.0 is a must-read for every educator! Paul and Barb help us realize the importance of understanding how to best support the needs of the whole child and how educators can work together to create a safe, collaborative environment and equitable approach to student learning."*

**—Jensen Ball**
consultant and manager, Hawaii State Department of
Education, Honolulu

*"In Leading Impact Teams 2.0, Paul and Barb offer essential information that can help students learn at high levels, while providing context in regard to this ever-changing world. By pairing the important instructional work of an educator with the equity issues we're tackling as a society, they provide a plan for all students, teachers, and families to become self-empowered learners."*

**—Steve Johnson**
director of consolidated programs,
Panama-Buena Vista Union School District,
and former principal of Highgate Elementary School,
Panama-Buena Vista Union School District,
Bakersfield, California

*"What a substantive and resource-filled text with oodles of videos and scaffolds, protocols, and practical pieces to use immediately in your support of*

*introducing, sustaining, and thriving in an Impact Team! This new edition has so much more to learn from—packed with new information and so much more for us to develop our collective efficacy on our teams and, in doing so, provide us direction and guidance to help us do what is best for our students."*

**—Jennifer Abrams**
communications consultant
and author of *Stretching Your Learning Edges: Growing (Up) at Work* (2021) and *Having Hard Conversations* (2009),
Palo Alto, California

*"Bloomberg and Pitchford have written a deeply practical and inspiring book about the impact that's possible with teacher teaming and collaboration, done right—while managing to expertly weave the all-important equity lens throughout. Their insights are sure to revolutionize this field."*

**—Jennifer Brown**
best-selling author *How to Be an Inclusive Leader: Your Role in Creating Cultures of Belonging Where Everyone Can Thrive* (2022),
Woodstock, New York

*"Collaboration does not come easy to most of us because of differing perspectives, a lack of an understanding of the ultimate goal for the group, and a belief that their voices do not matter. In Leading Impact Teams: Building a Culture of Efficacy and Agency, Bloomberg and Pitchford focus on helping to change those barriers into strengths, and they offer a great balance between research and practice."*

**—Peter DeWitt, EdD**
leadership coach, facilitator, author,
and director of the Educational Leadership Collective,
Albany, New York

*"Leading Impact Teams 2.0 is the ultimate guide for leveraging efficacy and agency for impact. Bloomberg and Pitchford provide a groundbreak-*

ing resource that reveals practical tools, strategies, and actions teams can take to ensure progress for all. A must-read for those passionate about creating meaningful change and ensuring collective efforts make a real difference."

**—Sarah Martin**
founding principal, Stonefields School, Auckland, New Zealand

"Leading Impact Teams 2.0 is the book every school and district needs if they want support for collaborative teacher teams—and it's still amazing with this updated release! As a practitioner who has worked with PLCs and struggled to find a way to make the work authentic and actionable, I say look no further. Bloomberg and Pitchford offer blueprint processes that come from decades of success moving learning forward across the nation. Their process provides step-by-step action to accelerate learning all while building learner agency for both students and teachers—the ultimate efficacy builder for all."

**—Dr. Jeanette Westfall**
coauthor *Learner Agency: A Field Guide for Taking Flight* (2023, with Kara Vandas and Ashley Duvall), Liberty, Missouri

"This new and improved Impact Teams is a must-have and a must-read for leaders looking for a humanistic approach to leading change. The content is both timely and relevant and makes the important learning illustrated in the book actionable. At a time when leaders are facing unparalleled challenges, Impact Teams delivers a compelling playbook fueled by data and purpose. This book offers enormous value for all stakeholders, without losing what's most important: the student in all of us."

**—Talonya Geary**
author, speaker, and talent enthusiast, New York, New York

"As a teacher, curriculum specialist, and professional developer, I felt stuck with PLCs. We spent copious time unpacking standards that only resulted in more eduspeak without clarity for students. Although we became decent *writers of assessment items, I saw little change in instruction across class-rooms. Paul and Barb's approach to teaming is tangible, actionable, and "doable" within real educator time. Teams gain clarity on student success criteria, write formative tasks with clear scaffolding options, and proactively move all students toward and beyond proficiency. Our experiences have increased collective efficacy and shifted mindsets for impactful formative instruction practices. Any teams wanting to impact student learning and make collaboration more efficient should dive into the Impact Teams model."*

**—Kate Canine**
director of professional learning, Poudre School District, Fort Collins, Colorado

*"As the principal of a large, urban school, I wanted my teachers to be energized by the work of their PLCs because of the impact on their students. I knew intuitively the weekly, and sometimes daily, collaboration had to be simple and purposeful while ultimately transforming teaching and learning. I heard Barb Pitchford speak at a principal's academy and felt like a kid in a candy store! Barb graciously accepted the invitation to work with me and my faculty using the Impact Teams Model. Quite humbly, we were transformed in ways we never thought possible, which led to transforming experiences for our students. Paul and Barb gave us an incredible gift by helping us operationalize PLCs using protocols and our own expertise. I am personally indebted to both of them for their genuine and honest approach to what I consider some of the most important work being done in education today."*

**—Tami Bird**
former principal, Rose Creek Elementary and Antelope Canyon Elementary, West Jordan, Utah

*"Leading Impact Teams 2.0, by Bloomberg and Pitchford, masterfully integrates the crucial concept of equity into the important work of teacher teams in our schools. Their insightful exploration of how equity in education can be woven into educational practices that transform teacher prac-*

*tice creates systems to enhance alignment to the formative assessment process. Through a blend of research, case studies in schools all over the country, and practical protocols, the authors illustrate how educators can create an inclusive environment where every student's unique needs are met. This book is a valuable resource for all educators who understand the value of collective efficacy and are invested in creating classrooms that are student driven."*

**—Hanin Hasweh**
principal, Harbor View School – PS59, Staten Island, New York

*"Leading Impact Teams 2.0 is a must-read, must-practice guide for leaders at any level (district, school, classroom) seeking to transform traditional PLCs into impactful teaching and learning teams by bolstering student agency and building a culture of collective teacher efficacy, all the while growing ubiquitous instructional leadership throughout your system! The Impact Team Model (ITM) has provided our district with the necessary structures, protocols, and supports needed to integrate some of Hattie's highest-yield influences on student learning into our Teaching and Learning Team (PLC) process, resulting in increased student learning and achievement, even during the school years most impacted by the pandemic. We now look forward to using this second edition as one of our core instructional mentor texts!"*

**—Dr. Angela Lyon Hinton**
assistant superintendent for instructional services, Spartanburg School District 2, Inman, South Carolina

*"Seldom does a book come along that inspires action and provides models, success criteria, and an abundance of resources to make it happen. Bloomberg and Pitchford breathe life into this process by making it timely and practical as well as providing the support needed to take it from theory to action. This revision leans into culturally responsive and sustaining practices and contains equity reflections throughout that challenge educators to examine our biases and move us toward the implementation of asset-based pedagogies. This is more than just a book about Impact Teams;*

*it is a step-by-step guide to transforming your traditional PLCs into stu-dent-centered teams with empowered learning for all at its heart."*

**—Rachel Carrillo Fairchild**
author of *How to Reach and Teach English Language Learners* (2011)
and *Common Formative Assessments for English Language Learners* (2014)
and coauthor of *Engaged Instruction: Thriving Classrooms in the Age of the
Common Core* (2013), *Peer Power* (2019) and *Amplify Learner Voice
through Culturally Responsive and Sustaining Assessment* (2023),
Driftwood, Texas

*"Leading Impact Teams 2.0 will help schools and teams get to the heart of
student achievement. This practical read helps teams build systems and
structures that make data analysis and, more importantly, "using" data
effectively to improve learning. Bloomberg and Pitchford have simplified
the process and made learning visible, helping teacher teams craft experiences based on data to support the growth of student skills. I highly recommend this read and the impact team process."*

**—Starr Sackstein**
consultant, COO of Mastery Portfolio,
author of *Hacking Assessment* (2022) and *Assessing with Respect*
(2021), Seminole, Florida

*"Impact Teams 2.0 has remodeled the roadmap for educators who are
truly wanting to make a difference within their PLC time and see the
IMPACT on student learning. Teacher and school demands, with initiative
fatigue and turnover, are ever-increasing. This book makes it manageable
to tackle those tough problems and dig deep into the inquiry process. For
the past 8 years, East Central BOCES has been participating in the Impact
Team Model, and this book gives us new and exciting research to help us
continue to grow and improve in our practice. Paul and Barb's profound
understanding of equity, collective teacher efficacy, Visible Learning, and
asset-based pedagogy shines through on every page."*

**—Megan Eikleberry**
East Central BOCES staff developer and Impact Team coach,
Strasbury, Colorado

*"Leading Impact Teams 2.0 is a great resource for anyone who is interested in invigorating their PLC process and empowering teachers to lead their own learning. The organization of the protocols in the new edition, particularly with a focus on advancing equity, ensures that students and evidence of learning are at the forefront of all of our conversations. The addition of protocols being implemented at a variety of school sites and grade levels is a great addition to this edition as they are the first thing our teachers always ask for."*

**—Brian Schum**
associate principal of curriculum and instruction, Lammersville Unified School District–Mountain House High School, Modesto, California

*"Leading Impact Teams 2.0 is an energizing read for instructional leaders interested in systematically transforming the mindset around growth and learning for all. The authors place an intentional focus on educational equity and the importance of relationships as the foundation for all within a system. The consistent approach to using the "Evidence–Analysis–Action" framework reshapes team conversations to collective problem-solving opportunities, where ideas are generated and strategically selected based on the evidence collected. This book truly reinforces the importance of creating a culture where learning for all is valued and the partnership between teachers and students is prioritized."*

**—Michelle Augustyniak**
associate principal of instruction, Amos Alonzo Stagg High School, Palos Hills, Illinois

*"Leading Impact Teams 2.0 sheds the anchor of traditional PLC processes with a contemporary take that is both inclusive and cogent. In this new book, Paul and Barb lead educators through the architecture of Impact Teams, a roadmap for educational leaders, teachers, and essential stakeholders. Not only do they explore the traditional tenets of PLCs, co-constructed with contemporary thought partners, but they explore equity, relationships, voice, and the affective domain that is the lynchpin to sustained organizational change. I look forward to sharing Impact Teams 2.0*

*with my team."*

—**Thorsten Harrison**
associate superintendent, Lammersville Unified School
District, Mountain House, California

*"Leading Impact Teams: Building a Culture of Efficacy and Agency is a must-read for school leaders looking to transform their educational institutions. This edition provides essential insights on the role of collective efficacy and team-building strategies to maximize the potential of your school leadership teams. The authors' focus on equity and effective communication provides the tools to foster a culture of trust and inclusivity, ensuring that every member of the school community can thrive. In partnership with The Core Collaborative, our region began this work with school teams and content-specific educator huddles a year ago, and we have already seen exciting transformations of instruction and classroom cultures that are fostering self-empowered learners."*

—**Jennifer Teeter**
IMESD/OTREN instructional coach, InterMountain Education
Service District, Pendleton, Oregon

*"Prepare to embark on a profound educational journey with this exceptional book. It's a compelling exploration of Impact Teams 2.0 that seamlessly combines the essential elements of student learner agency, equity, asset-based models, and humanizing pedagogy. In a world craving innovation and purpose, this book is a beacon for educators seeking to empower their students and transform their practice. It's a visionary guide for shaping a brighter future in education."*

—**Vivett Dukes**
Career-Educator and Author, New York, New York

*"Leading Impact Teams offers a great blend of rationale, research, and doable application. Effectively organized in a recurring format that includes the what, why, and how of the topic in focus, each chapter con-*

*cludes with a nutshell summary, a check-in reader assessment and related implementation activity, along with teacher-voice tips and testimonials in print and video formats. What's unique and noteworthy in this book is its powerful set of collaborative protocols focused on evidence, analysis, and action that puts students at the center of the teaching and learning process. This clearly reflects the authors' stated ultimate goal: 'for students to be able to independently assess their own learning."*

**—Larry Ainsworth**
Author of *Common Formative Assessments 2.0*

*"Leading Impact Teams offers one of the most thoughtful, powerful, and purposeful books in a long time that holds the potential to both catalyze and transform educational systems. Through an immensely enjoyable read, Bloomberg and Pitchford provide an accessible and easy-to-follow roadmap to the complex journey of building efficacy and teams. This book is a must read for educators and policy makers who are committed to bringing out the best in systems, students, and communities."*

**—Professor Alan J. Daly**
University of California, San Diego

# LEADING IMPACT TEAMS

# LEADING IMPACT TEAMS

## Building a Culture of Efficacy and Agency

**Paul Bloomberg**

**Barb Pitchford**

*Forewords by John Hattie and Alan J. Daly*

*Author Contributions*
*Dr. Michael De Sousa • Isaac Wells • Sarah Stevens • Katherine Smith*

MIMI & TODD
— PRESS —

This Mimi & Todd Press, Inc. second edition September 2023

For information about special discounts for bulk purchases, or other inquiries, please contact Mimi & Todd Press, Inc. Sales at info@mimitoddpress.com or 1090 N. Palm Canyon Drive, Suite B, Palm Springs, CA 92262.

ISBN:     978-1-950089-18-5 (paperback)
          978-1-950089-19-2 (e-book)

Publishing Coordinator: Bart Harvey
Program Director: Paul Bloomberg
Publishing Manager: Tony Francoeur
Copy/Line Editor: Jennifer Z. Marshall
Art Director & Designer: Alison Cox
Indexer: Maria Sosnowski
Marketing Lead: Jace McCracken

**Download Impact Teams digital resources:**
https://qrco.de/LeadingImpactTeamsResources

# Contents

# Foreword

## Know thy Impact

Teacher collective efficacy is the latest hot topic among educators—collaborating to build confidence and boost student learning progress. In 2011, Rachel Eells placed it among the most powerful influences on student learning, with an effect size of 1.36 (Hattie, 2023). Teachers' collective efficacy requires working together, building a mindset that all students can make appreciable progress, and reinforcing this belief with evidence. Students do indeed learn by these teachers "causing learning."

*Leading Impact Teams: Building a Culture of Efficacy and Agency* combines some of the best innovations from the last decade. It ensures a focus on changing students' learning lives. Like all good cake recipes, it is not just the ingredients but how we mix them—with the tender, loving care illustrated throughout these chapters. The key to this book's success: building a culture of efficacy in leaders, teachers, and students by developing Impact Teams.

To enable teachers to understand, build confidence in growth, and feed this confidence with evidence requires a determined, focused, and knowledgeable leader. It needs space, resources, and time to occur, to ensure implementation, and to evaluate impact. This book outlines the themes. Then we collect evidence, form professional learning communities, and work together to interpret the impact of our teaching on each and every student. This interpretation is the core notion of clinical practice in most professions. It contrasts the usual life of teachers—working alone (but often sitting together), closed classroom doors, discussions reserved for anecdotes, selective memories about what works, and designing pre-specific engagement activities to keep students on target until the bell rings. This book focuses more on the activities' consequences, the magnitude of growth, collaboration to maximize impact, and sharing with colleagues, students, families, and the community.

Such methods require high levels of trust, a notion this book often references. In some of my team's work, trust-building can take months before we can build teams that develop high levels of efficacy. Teachers and schools have been so bashed in the past decades that they feel appropriately nervous about sharing data and evidence—it has often been used against them. Instead, we premise this book on the considerable success all around us in schools. We ask how we can reliably identify this expertise, use it in Impact Teams, then develop and share it. Such scaling is the ever-charging battery in this process.

This book asks us all to reconsider setting up another team, yet again looking at data and arranging another professional learning community. Instead, let's laser focus on the *purposes* of these communities—to maximize impact on student learning *together*. We need to use evidence when making impactful decisions. This book creates a forum for a formative evaluation of student work and other pertinent sources of evidence, helping students plan the next steps while assisting teachers with guiding them toward success criteria.

Of course, I am delighted they use my synthesis of meta-analyses to inform the book's claims. It took me 15 years to write the first Visible Learning book related to creating the underlying story. Gathering data is the easier part. It takes more work to interpret it and check that others understand it. Similarly, throughout this book, Bloomberg and Pitchford emphasize data interpretation, shape interpretations, and provide opportunities to check them for veracity and impact. Building the story about the data is more critical than the data. That makes this book successful in the same way that interpreting student learning evidence helps teachers succeed.

My theme centers on maximizing impact, requiring robust discussions in educational settings about our collective understanding of impact. Learning progressions should not rely on the particular beliefs of any one teacher. It should come from all student encounters in a school. It is more than scores on tests. We invite students to participate in learning. We involve the joy of learning and taking on challenges. We know when students successfully learn. We discover sufficient trial pathways to solutions. We attain precious knowledge. Michael Young's claims continually remind me that such attainment includes providing students with the knowledge they would not have without attending school.

Maximizing this impact involves teachers learning from students about their impact—the heart of formative evaluation—the substance of collaborative inquiry among teacher teams. This demands instructional leaders to hone the purpose, build trust, and ensure quality communication. This demands high social sensitivity to others, respect for evidence, and beliefs that everyone can cause learning. All these lie at the core of Bloomberg and Pitchford's Impact Team Model.

They outline the *what*, *why*, and *how* aspects of building these teams, continually providing evidence as feedback, reflections on the sufficiency of the impact considering the time and energies imparted, and ensuring they put the evidence into action. In the Impact Teams cycle—and it is a virtuous circle—evidence and analysis drive actions that loop back into the team, ultimately benefiting the students. Oh, and it supports teachers, as one of the major reasons we are in this business is to impact all students!

**John Hattie**

# Foreword

## Re-visiting the Relational Impact of Impact Teams

I write these words in Abiquiu New Mexico—my newly adopted second home. Abiquiu is a beautiful rural place in Northern New Mexico. I find myself here as a way to occasionally escape the increasing pressure of urbanity in which one is both simultaneously surrounded and often desperately isolated—not so different from what a typical educator might feel in a school or district. As I write these words and reflect on *Impact Teams* a question arises for me around how do we re-awaken the relational and authentic parts of ourselves to truly engage—to become a *part* of when so much presses us to be *apart from*. After re-reading *Impact Teams* I recognize that at the work's heart beats the importance of relational rhythms and connection—something that is near and dear to my own heart. It is in this context, coupled with being deeply inspired and reenergized by Paul and Barb's work, that I write this prologue. Reconnecting with our shared humanity and interdependence is no longer background, rather it is *the* space in which we need to be critically engaging in thoughtful, intentional, and strategic ways and *Impact Teams* offers us an invigorating opportunity to re-consideration our own important work.

Although I was likely invited to provide this prologue as a way to reflect on my own work around networks and collaboration over the last decade and a half, I will use my few pages as an opportunity to reflect on the larger world and our shared collective experiences as we move forward into this exciting new space Paul and Barb are revisiting in this powerful work. *Impact Teams* from my vantage point simultaneously deepens and expands the important work around collaboration and efficacy and brings to life through research, practice, and deep insights renewed ways of engaging. I would like to also note that I am personally and professionally indebted to Paul and Barb as this piece is inspired not only by the excellent literature, thoughtful writing, and compelling arguments in this book, but for the real work they both have contributed over the years which has influenced my thinking and being in so many ways. Paul and Barb are the rare combination of scholars/practitioners that can beautifully and meaningfully link research to practice and back again. I have chosen to take a decidedly more personal voice as I think we all need to take a breath and deeply consider ourselves beyond labels and positions, reflect on our shared humanity, and contemplate what comes next. I am hopeful my words will catalyze a larger reflective dialogue about our interactional spaces both now and into the future.

## Re-Envisioning

We must recognize the economic, emotional, and physical bandwidth necessary to survive and engage with others in this modern time and make a significant recommitment to equitable economic, health, education, and well-being outcomes. To varying degrees, we experience strained discourse and discord as we find ourselves in a quickly changing and seemingly more divisive world that is in need of healing and restorative practices. We, as a society, seem less prepared or maybe less willing to handle disruption and differing perspectives, and perhaps it was less about the system failing, as some would argue the system has been failing for years, but more that we had no coherent, compassionate, and collaborative system in place to respond to deep disruption.

We are searching for answers in a rapidly evolving space which may result in increases in emotional distress, and social isolation, but also deeply questioning the status quo. Perhaps because of this disruption we have also been granted a moment to engage in more productive and constructive patterns of interactions with one another—to reconsider our impact on each other and our planet. We have an opportunity to push beyond technical solutions to take a more human-centered design approach to what the future may look like and how education might reimagine itself. How can we rebuild and reimagine educational systems in support of the larger public good in ways that center humanity and embrace intersectionality in all its forms? To do so requires us to reconnect in a spirit of hope, trust, and compassionate empathy toward one another. Absent this rethinking it is unclear to me we can reach the horizon of hope and impact that Paul and Barb write about so passionately.

## Re-Connecting

We on this planet are interdependent with our interdependence stretching out beyond our awareness. Actions in distant places, as well as in our own neighborhoods and schools, have the potential to impact our sense of purpose and well-being. We have always been aware of the fact that we live in a small world. Recall your surprise when a random person you met in an airport knows a relative of yours. Now, however, our interdependence is front and center and demands our constant attention and most importantly our care. A wide range of scientific disciplines have argued in one way or another about the significance of our interconnectivity ranging from philosophy to ecology, to biology to sociology, and to the growing work around networks referenced in *Impact Teams*.

In many ways the ideas of interconnection and networks are both a scientific reality and, now more than ever, an increasing metaphor about the way we live our lives. It is becoming even more clear that we as humans are powerfully and inescapably interconnected. We are all deeply entwined, and while recent global pandemic and pain may be the most salient reminder of that connection, we now also have the chance to reconnect to dormant values around connection, community, care, and collaboration. Perhaps in this new period of relational re-awakening, we may rediscover the best in ourselves and do so by realizing that each of our interactions are imbued with meaning, possibility, and hope. During this time, we have come to realize we are all wonderfully fragile and desperately human and that realization may portend the greatest catalyzer for change and potential for impact.

## Re-Thinking

We have an opportunity to collectively call into question basic ideas about the way we have constructed our world. One such example is how we measure and determine 'productivity'. The industrialization of the workplace and school systems has attuned us to the idea of time clocks and punching in and out of work. Your value and pay were (are) tied to your productivity, which was effectively measured in minutes, hours, and days. Hours dedicated to work became the default measurement of value and productivity. This notion and way of being still remain very much in place in work; even within schools. However, in the new reality of working and what it means to be a contributing member of society, the rather blunt measure of productivity in terms of hours spent has likely well outlived its usefulness. Perhaps the better measure is one around overall output, impact, and supporting the flourishing of self and others.

The shift to output and well-being as a measure of productivity will be challenging as so many systems have been built up around the counting of hours. Our educational systems were designed to produce knowledge and workers for industry, but if we are to truly progress we need to embrace the gifts of reimagination and the potential of human-based systems of impact. Systems that live into the powerful approach of, "With Us, For Us, By Us", hold potential to transform education in a diverse society. This transition to a more socially connected output/well-being-valued approach will require changes in how we relate and higher levels of relational trust between and among community members—simply put we will need to reimagine how we consider impact as we see in the pages that follow this forward.

We know that systems with lower levels of trust have higher transaction costs. These costs are reflected in increased policies, rules, and regulations and the need for higher accountability and more technical engagement. High-trust systems engender a sense of belonging and efficacy and are built on a foundation that recognizes individual and collective contributions. A meaningful contribution supports goals much larger than oneself—relational trust fosters well-being, resilience, and the ability to adapt to changing contexts—exactly what is needed in reimagined relational spaces that have real impact. As such, supporting and creating high-trust relational systems is one of the core conditions necessary to transition to new and different types of interactions outlined in this book.

## Re-Orienting

Lifting up one's head reminds us of the myriad examples of artists, musicians, storytellers, playwrights, intellectuals, yoga teachers, and a host of generous and gracious others who gift their talents to the world and provide experiences and impact for many who would otherwise be left out. This orientation towards others reflects a life of awareness and giving to others in the spirit of the public good—a core value of *Impact Teams*. It reminds me of what it takes to live, learn, and love in a rural community. The opportunity to ask "what can I offer" and how can I be a resource for others is rooted in compassion, kindness, generosity, and empathy for the world. This idea reflects and acknowledges that we each have a story, a gift, a contribution to make to the many pressing needs of the world no matter our background, experience, or perspective. Opportunities to build and nurture social capital and community reflect our best and the insights contained within this book help bring this to life.

I remain hopeful we will take the time to re-build, re-imagine, and re-tool our societies and educational systems and focus on significant investments in the global public good. Rather than pull back further into our individualistic shells, we have the opportunity to become even more communal and better linked. The frameworks and approaches outlined in *Impact Teams* will have an important role to play, and if considered deeply, expand our notions of even deeper impact. Our collective experiences around the pandemic are proof we are vulnerable and exposed as a species. We will need a collective response from all sectors, especially education, to begin to pose, address and understand risks and responses to the challenges and solutions of a planet-wide event and to critically question and act upon long-held structural inequities. The time for action is now and reconsidering our relational impact holds important potential and possibility as we move into an even more hopeful and reimagined educational space.

**Alan J. Daly**
**Abiquiu, New Mexico**
**August 2023**

# Acknowledgments

We didn't achieve this success alone. When we were asked whom to acknowledge for this book, the first thing that came out of both of our mouths was "our partner districts, schools, teachers, and students!" This book simply would not have happened without the many thought partners we have worked with over the past several years who were willing to take risks with us and who believe what we believe in. We are deeply indebted to the students, the teachers, and the leaders who worked with us to develop the Impact Team Model.

Thank you to the following thought partners:

- St. Claire Adriaan, Principal and Consultant, California
- Louise Alfano, Former Principal, PS 112, District 20, and her team of dedicated teachers-leaders.
- Lisa Arcuri, Principal, PS 5, District 20, NYC DOE, and her team of dedicated teachers
- Stephanie Bargone and Nicole Hughes PS9, District 31, NYC DOE
- Tami Bird, Principal (retired), Jordan School District, West Jordan, Utah
- Eric Bloomberg, Linked In, Chicago, IL
- Donna Bonanno, PS 60, District 31, NYC DOE and her team of dedicated teachers-leaders.
- John Boyle, Principal, Totten Intermediate School, District 31, NYC DOE, and his dedicated team of teachers
- Jamie Bronuskas, Science Teacher, Lyons Township High School District 204, La Grange, IL
- Joanne Buckheit, Principal, Petrides K-12, District 31, NYC DOE and her team of dedicated teachers

- Kate Canine, Director of Professional Services, Poudre School District, Ft. Collins, CO
- Graziela Casale and Lauren Stasio PS9, District 31, NYC DOE
- Center for Innovative Teaching and Learning at Northern Illinois University
- Christine Chavez, Deputy Superintendent, District 31, NYC DOE
- The fifth grade at PS 20, The Christy J. Cugini Port Richmond School, District 31, Staten Island, NY
- Virginia Condon, American studies teacher, Lyons Township High School District 204, La Grange, IL
- Jodi Contento, Principal, PS 78, District 31, NYC DOE and her team of dedicated teachers
- Center for the Collaborative Classroom, Alameda, CA
- The Core Collaborative, National Impact Team Coaches, Palm Springs, CA
- Christy J. Cugini, Port Richmond School, PS 20, District 31, NYC DOE
- Alan Daly, Professor and Chair, Department of Education Studies at University of California, San Diego
- Sharon Daxton-Vorce, former Coordinator of Professional Learning, EC BOCES, CO
- Danielle Di Capua, Teacher Leader, PS 22, District 31, NYC DOE
- Melissa Donnath, Principal, PS 22, District 31, NYC DOE and her team of dedicated teachers
- Vivett Dukes, Author and Consultant, Queens, NY
- Jason Ericson, PE Teacher, PS 9, District 31, NYC DOE
- Mark Erlenwein, Principal, Staten Island Tech, District 31, NYC DOE and his team of dedicated teachers
- Gina Ferguson, Instructional Coach and Consultant, Kennewick, WA
- Melissa Garofalo and Erin O'Hanlon, PS 35, District 31, NYC DOE, and her team of dedicated teachers
- Vincenza Gallasio, Former Superintendent, District 31, NYC DOE

- Michelle Harbin, Chemistry Teacher, Lyons Township High School District 204, La Grange, IL
- Cheryle Lerch, District Administrator, Fort Bend ISD, Sugar Land, TX
- Anthony Lodico, Former Executive Superintendent of District 31, NYC DOE
- Christine Loughlin, Former Superintendent of District 3, NYC DOE
- Susi Mauldin, 6th grade communication arts teacher, Reeds Spring School District, Reeds Spring, MO
- Courtney McGinn and Jessica Vigliotti, ICT Teachers, PS 45, District 31, NYC DOE
- Lora McKillop, Principal of Oakland Elementary School, Spartanburg, SC
- James Milkert, World History Teacher, Lyons Township High School District 204, La Grange, IL
- Lyons Township High School Administration in La Grange, IL, with special thanks to the first 10 Model Impact Teams, Alyssa Brands, Virginia Condon, Michelle Harbin, and James Milkert for recording their efforts implementing the EAA Classroom Protocol, and Kurt Johns, Sue McClenahan, and Susie Murphy for sharing their collaborative inquiry
- Rhonda McCellan, Instructional Coach, Amistad Elementary, Kennewick, WA
- Deanna Marco, Principal, PS 9, District 31, NYC DOE, and her team of dedicated teachers
- Paul Martuccio, Principal, PS 13, District 31, NYC DOE, and his team of dedicated teachers
- Lori McCord, Former Principal, Kennewick, WA and her admin and coaching team
- Michael McDowell, Author and Consultant, The Core Collaborative, San Rafael, CA
- Chantel Mebane, Administrator of Curriculum & Instruction, Norris School District, Bakersfield, CA
- Kelly Miller, Superintendent (retired), Norris School District, Bakersfield, California

- Dawn Minutelli, Director of Curriculum and Assessment, and her team at Santee Unified School District in Santee, CA
- Julie Munn and her team at Kelsey Norman Elementary, Joplin Schools, Joplin, MO
- Chris Ogno, Former Principal, PS 247, District 20, NYC DOE, and his team of dedicated assistant principals and teachers
- Gabriella Pasquale and Lana Regenbogen, ICT teachers, PS 5, NYC DOE
- Jeneca Parker-Tongue, Founding Director, Center for Social and Emotional Learning, Hunter College, New York
- Kelly Pease, Director of Intervention Services, Lake Washington School District, Redmond, Washington
- Julio Blanco Pena and Natalie Lahti, Leadership, Amistad Elementary, Kennewick, WA and their team of dedicated teachers
- Susan Perez, Former Assistant Superintendent, Pajaro Unified School District, Watsonville, CA
- Karen Raino, EL and ELA Division Chair at Lyons Township High School District 204, La Grange, IL
- Michelle Ramos, PS 16, District 31 and her team of dedicated leaders and teachers
- Guillermo Ramos, Mike Nebesnick, and Hilda Aguirre, Middle School Principals, Gilroy Unified, CA
- Lana Regenbogen and Gabriella Pasquale, PS 5, NYC DOE
- Marisol Queveda Rerucha, Author and Consultant, San Diego, CA
- The National Equity Project
- Starr Sackstein, Author and Consultant, The Core Collaborative, Chief Operating Officer at Mastery Portfolio, Seminole, FL
- Samantha Sahota, 2nd Grade Teacher, PS 9, District 31, NYC DOE
- Sarah Stevens, Executive Director of Quality Implementation, The Core Collaborative
- Hope Strasser, Former Teaching & Learning Coach, Kelsey Norman Elementary, Joplin, MO

- Chris Templeton, Former President, Learning Forward MO
- Dayna Ugo, math teacher, IS 34, NYC DOE
- Kara Vandas, Author and Consultant, Colorado
- Debra Vigstom, Principal, Highland High School, Kern High School District, Bakersfield, CA
- Dr. Brian Waterman, superintendent of Lyons Township High School District 204, La Grange, IL
- Jennifer Wildman, former Superintendent of Mammoth Unified School District, Mammoth Lakes, CA
- Marion Wilson, Superintendent, District 31, NYC DOE

Thank you to Kristin Anderson, for taking a chance on us. In one conversation in 2016, she framed our message and strengthened our work around our profound belief—that when teachers believe they can make a difference for ALL students, they actually do!

Finally, we would like to say a special thank you to John Hattie and Alan Daly, who guided our work and who wrote the Forewords to this book. Their research has inspired us to truly make a difference!

## From Barb Pitchford

We didn't choose each other, the work chose for us. However it happened, I am thankful for the most talented and brilliant writing partner on the planet. I now realize that having a writing partner is a bit like a marriage—many challenges, non-stop learning, and so cool to have someone to share the successes with. Special thanks to my children, Molly and Scott, who have always hung in there with me even when they had to spend many long days at school with me. And to my family and friends who know and understand my passion for the work and are there to cheer me on but also to remind me about this thing called "balance"—to go for a hike or ride my horse. And to the many teachers and administrators who have worked with me over the years – you have been my most powerful teachers!

## From Paul Bloomberg

I am truly grateful for my amazing writing partner, friend, coach and confidante, Barb Pitchford. We have been on quite a journey since 2014 (it is hard to believe). We continue to strive to ensure that students, families and educators remain at the center while writing this book and through developing the Impact Team Model. There is no greater gift than when people take ownership of their learning, mistakes and all.

A special thanks to my parents, Jon and Marilyn Bloomberg, who always kept me focused on setting goals and being mindful of others. They urged me to make a "dent in the world" by making a positive difference in the lives of other people. Talonya, one of my many students and my sister—she taught me how to truly partner with students, and now we have been best friends for over 25 years. Alex and Taylor, my sons, have taught me how important it is for students to take ownership of their learning. Mimi Aronson, my mentor and hero, taught me to always trust students to lead the way, and they never have let me down. Tony, my husband, believes in this work as much as Barb and I do, and we love him for his unwavering support, his sacrifice, and dedication to making a difference in the lives of others.

## Publisher's Acknowledgments

Mimi & Todd Press gratefully acknowledges the contributions of the following people:

- Bart Harvey, Publishing Coordinator
- Alison Cox, Creative Director
- Donnie Luehring, Video Support
- Andrea Orduna, Creative Assistant
- Jace McCracken, Marketing
- Kenna Combs, Learning Network Specialist
- Leah Tierney, Business Lead
- Brian Roy, Executive Director of Learning Partnerships

# About the Authors

## Paul James Bloomberg, EdD

I am gay white man who grew up in a very remote part of Northern Michigan where I never felt I truly belonged. Growing up there were times when I didn't want to live and tried to change everything about who I was. In my early twenties, I slowly came out to my family and friends. Every time I "came out," I became more confident with my identity regardless of the outcome. However, when I began my career in public education, I didn't feel safe to show up to work as my authentic self. I didn't feel I could be open about my identity with my students, the families I served and many of the people I worked with. When I became a parent, I finally chose to show up as the real me, the whole me. If I hadn't, I would have continued to not just violate my own dignity but that of my family.

I am the proud husband of Tony Francoeur and the co-dad to Alex and Taylor, who have taught me more about humanity than my formal education ever could. Our sons never felt valued and honored as learners, especially in the secondary world of assessment-grading and reporting. Like most parents, Tony and I struggled with the school system and were not confident in how we supported them in school and in life. If I, as a celebrated educational leader, struggled to advocate for my own children, I could hardly imagine the experience of other parents. Tony and I knew we had to do something.

My parents, both nurses and advocates for the elderly, were also entrepreneurs. Tony and I harnessed our parents' honesty, belief in justice, unconditional love and their entrepreneurial spirit and decided to disrupt the educational landscape together and founded The Core Collaborative Learning Network, a network of educators dedicated to reimagining public education and the home of Impact Teams. To us, disrupting our educational system means that we must explore ways we can work against the racism of which white privilege is a cornerstone.

I'm so grateful that I finally began to show up in life as the real me. It is also with gratitude that I accept the white privilege I was born with and acknowledge the privileges I continue to benefit from as a white man. Accepting my privilege also means that I am responsible for partnering with others to organize and work to dismantle systems of oppression by creating conditions in our schools for self-empowerment. Collaboratively learning, writing and releasing this book with Barb, Michael, Isaac, Katie, Sarah and our partner schools is just one part of our collective journey to reimagine education.

# Barb Pitchford

My abrupt awakening of the vast and devastating world of inequities hit in 1971. Fresh out of college I was sent to an island in Alaska to be the high school counselor for 300 seniors, some just a few years younger than me. The Vietnam war was raging, teaching jobs were scarce, and I was a privileged white girl rebelling against the war, the bureaucracy, and the systems built decades ago to keep us all 'in our places'. Over 90% lived below the poverty line, over 50% were the indigenous peoples of the Pacific Northwest Coast (The Tlingit); most had never been off the island.

Being the "green" high school counselor for these extraordinary students changed not only my perspective but also the trajectory of my life. From that year on, the driving force in my life has been the belief that every, and I mean every child deserves to learn in a school that respects honors, values and affirms the life experiences, perspectives and needs that they bring into the classroom as vital assets and resources for learning. They deserve a culturally responsive, rigorous, education that challenges them to be critical thinkers and promotes learner agency so we end long standing inequities.

In the nearly 50 years I have been in education, I've been a teacher, counselor, administrator, and consultant pre-K – 12. I became a principal early on because I wanted the power to say "Yes, we can!". I was tired of hearing "No, we can't". Paul and I discovered each other when we were both newbies in the consulting field and fresh from public school administration. We both felt the same driving force to help schools have a positive impact on all students. We knew it was possible because we had both done it! We share(d) a bone deep belief that it is critical to build a school culture in which students and teachers have daily opportunities to be successful – to learn to believe in themselves as learners and as valuable contributors to their communities. Quite simply to thrive in a culture in which efficacy and agency are the cornerstones of learning.

I am forever grateful to have found Paul and like-minded colleagues who share the same passion, to be in service to all children.

## Dr. Michael J. De Sousa

Dr. Michael J. De Sousa, the founder of RODA Leadership Development, has a unique professional background, having served as a teacher, high school principal, executive leader, researcher, and community organizer. He is a first-generation college graduate who went on to earn a Master's and Doctorate in Education. He has been recognized for his transformative leadership in schools and his dedicated advocacy for underserved families. He aspires to uphold his immigrant parents' legacy and be an example for his three children.

# Isaac Wells

Isaac is the Director of Teaching and Learning with the Core Collaborative. During his career in public education, he taught Kindergarten, 2nd, 4th, and 5th grades and worked as a School Improvement Specialist and Instructional Coach. Isaac has a passion for the learning process and loves nothing more than to roll up his sleeves and work with other educators and their students. He is confident this updated edition of Leading Impact Teams: Building a Culture of Efficacy and Agency will have a deep and lasting impact on learning.

# Sarah Stevens

Sarah Stevens presently holds the role of executive director of quality implementation at The Core Collaborative. With over 20 years of experience, she has been a champion for school improvement and innovation her entire career. Sarah's experience spanning from classroom teaching to curriculum and assessment director roles, equips her with a deep understanding of the dynamics found in almost every educational institution.

Sarah is known for her ability to bridge the gap between theory and practice. In her current role, Sarah supports schools and district leaders by co-constructing goals for professional learning connected to their initiatives for continuous improvement. Sarah's commitment to educational equity is at the heart of her work, ensuring every student receives a high-quality education. Her leadership is characterized by fostering a culture of collaboration and innovation among educators to elevate teaching and learning. Sarah lives in the midwest with her husband, James, and their two children, Deagan and Bria.

# Katherine Smith

Katie is the Executive Director of Operations with The Core Collaborative. During her career in public education, she served as a Social Studies Teacher and Department Chair, Assistant Principal of Curriculum & Instruction, Professional Learning Team Leader, Instructional Coaching Program Supervisor, and District Coordinator of Assessment & Research. Katie has had the pleasure of supporting Impact Team implementation in a large suburban district. She is dedicated to actualizing the work described in this updated edition of Leading Impact Teams because she has witnessed its positive impact on systems, educators, and students.

# Introduction

As authors and school improvement coaches, we extend deep gratitude to Corwin Press for the inaugural publication of this book in 2017; it became a Corwin best-seller in only 3 months. We had no idea it would resonate with so many learning communities across the globe.

## We clearly didn't achieve this success alone.

We continue to honor John Hattie and his monumental contribution to the field of education. When serving as national Visible Learning coaches, we realized that the Visible Learning research validated what we already knew to be true. The greatest effects on student learning come when the students become their own teachers (through self-monitoring and self-assessment), and teachers become learners of their teaching by understanding their impact on students. This is still the mission of the Impact Team Model.

Impact Teams partner with students to advance learner agency so our learners develop the skills, knowledge, and dispositions to make decisions that support themselves while contributing positively to others. We realize this mission through asset-based, collaborative inquiry centered on quality, culturally responsive and sustaining formative assessment.

Professor Alan Daly, a mentor and friend from the University of California, San Diego, taught us about the power of quality relationships and connections in positive school transformation. Although this message seems intuitive, policymakers at all levels of education seem to disregard it.

Dan Alpert, our Corwin editor, and Kristin Anderson, former director of Corwin Professional Learning, tremendously supported our dream of writing our first book. We honor both of them with this new edition.

We piloted the Impact Team Model nationwide for 3 years before our first publication with Corwin. Seven years later, hundreds of schools have adopted the model. Their contributions have been integral to our collective success. Our national Impact Team coaches brought the model to life in schools nationwide. Their collective fingerprints cover this text. They continue to be our learning partners as we work to make this model even more sustainable.

In the spirit of Impact Teams, we collaborated with four other thought partners for this edition. You would not be reading this book if it weren't for Isaac Well's significant contributions. He is not only a wonderful thought partner, but he has a special way of helping you tap into your self-awareness. He uses his ability to listen and coach as a superpower, and we all benefit from his expertise. We have partnered with Katie Smith since the launch of our pilot at Lyons Township High School in La Grange, Illinois. Katie's expertise in systems thinking strengthened this model, and her work with secondary teachers inspires us. Dr. Michael De Sousa wrote our equity reflections and supported our development process. He facilitates personal and professional learning that always makes you feel valued and loved. His feedback and explanations make you feel closer to our shared humanity. Sarah Stevens, our director of quality implementation, has partnered with us the longest. Sarah's feedback, support, and belief in this model over the past decade have helped schools navigate and create personalized quality implementation plans for each specific system. Her ability to listen, nurture, and care for educators brought efficacy to the model. She is more than a friend and thought partner; she is our sister.

Tony Francoeur is a husband (Paul's), father, son, brother, and uncle. He is also the CFO of The Core Collaborative and Mimi & Todd Press. His Impact Team Model contributions can't be overstated. He has been with us from the inception, has done everything in his power to meet our needs, and has been our biggest cheerleader. He has traveled globally promoting this model and poured love, compassion, and sincerity into this work.

Corwin continued to successfully publish our book until the spring of 2023. At that point, we decided to bring *Leading Impact Teams* home to Mimi & Todd Press (MTP), the independent press company we (Paul and Tony) founded in 2018. We named MTP after two of Paul's friends and colleagues. Mimi was a New York City educator, mother, sister, aunt, grandmother, national writing coach, and a dear friend. She was family. She taught every educator in her presence to "actively listen" to students. She deeply knew that when you truly listen to students, they will always lead the way. Todd, a passionate and talented educator, partner, brother, uncle, son, and friend, didn't think his life had value because he was queer. Their contribution as educators will live on through the pages of all MTP books.

Like all Mimi & Todd books, we dedicate this book to educators, organizers, thought leaders, parents, friends, and mentors who continue to inspire us to be better educators and human beings.

## COMMITTING TO EQUITY

Education stands at an inflection point. The pandemic and large-scale protests for racial justice and civil rights catalyzed a rethinking of the purpose and practices of education. Our educational system has always been in crisis; these inequities have generationally existed. Our current educational system was not created to ensure that all students achieve highly. Our system focuses on competition, deficits, assimilation, and hierarchy. This constructed inequity results in academic disparities, generational poverty, the school-to-prison pipeline, and poor mental, physical, and emotional health. Marisol Quevedo Rerucha, author of *Beyond the Surface of Restorative Practices*, explains,

> *Why is equity needed? Our school systems were created to promote the ideals of white supremacy, leaving our students who are Black, Brown, Indigenous, low-income, disabled, English*

*Learner, with learning disabilities, identify as LGBT+, and those unhoused or in foster care, without the access, opportunity, and sense of belonging of their mainstream white peers. Equity is not a destination. It is a journey that includes institutional reckoning and transformation. (Bloomberg et al., 2022, p. XIV)*

Rerucha designed Figure 0.1 to illustrate our nation's schools' generational and ongoing inequity.

**Figure 0.1: Systemic Harm**

**The Problem**

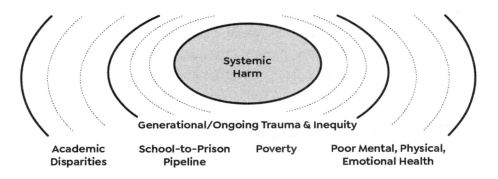

Rerucha explains, "The transformation of our system for seven generations can only happen when we accept the reality of why and how the system was formed and how it has harmed centuries of students." (Bloomberg et al., 2022, p. XIII) Along with Rerucha, we urge educators to transform the systems that created these long-standing inequities.

## What Do We Mean by Equity?

Equity is fair treatment, access, opportunity, and advancement for all people while striving to identify and eliminate barriers that prevent their full participation. Improving equity involves increasing justice and fairness within the practices and policies of institutions and systems. Tackling equity issues requires understanding the root causes of outcome disparities within our society.

We seek to advance culturally responsive and sustaining education practices by reimagining formative assessment through an asset-based cultural lens. To us, this means acknowledging and valuing people's diverse experiences and expertise as a source of knowledge. It includes acknowledging the context in which our students, families, and educators operate and the histories of the communities we aim to support.

In our latest book, *Amplify Learner Voice through Culturally Responsive and Sustaining Assessment*, we describe what H. Richard Milner (2020) calls the *opportunity gap.*

> *Millions of students are being negatively impacted by what H. Richard Milner (2020) calls the opportunity gap. The opportunity gap is a way to explain how social or economic factors—like race, language, gender, economic, and family situations—can influence whether individuals can reach their educational goals, career prospects, and other life aspirations. It focuses on the inputs rather than the outputs that often influence or determine a child's opportunities in life. The opportunity gap allows us to focus on how we as a system can improve and how the gaps we witness result from not providing the same opportunities for all students to succeed and thrive.*
>
> *The opportunity gap pushes us to acknowledge that our current educational system is flawed and perpetuates inequitable learning and assessment practices.*
>
> (Bloomberg et al., 2022, pp. 7–8)

In Leading Impact Teams 2.0, we focus on what's within our control as practitioners. We urge you to reimagine formative assessment and effective teaming practices through an asset-based, culturally responsive lens. Asset-based pedagogy focuses on recognizing and leveraging the strengths, talents, experiences, and cultural backgrounds that students, families, and educators bring to the learning community, rather than focusing on their deficits or challenges. Exchanging deficit-thinking and actions for asset-based approaches is within the control of every learner.

## LET'S LEARN TOGETHER

We all learn through experimentation, practice (and more practice), and sharing with one another. We have invited our partner districts, schools, teachers, and students to write their success stories! Each story is unique, but all share the same foundation: the basics of the Impact Team Model.

Impact Teams create the culture and conditions for every teacher daily to answer the question: "What is my impact?" Impact Teams reenergize teacher teams to believe in their collective capacity to make a difference, to immediately and significantly increase student and teacher learning.

## What's New:

- A focus on equity and the infusion of asset-based pedagogies
- An emphasis on the role of efficacy in cultivating learner agency
- Updated *Visible Learning* effect sizes
- Updated videos that directly connect to our *Core Collaborative YouTube Channel*
- A focus on social network theory to support innovation
- A stronger look at quality implementation based on partnering with over 500 schools and systems
- Access to our updated protocol handbook via QR code in the online appendix
- QR code access to our new *Impact Team Website* in the online appendix. (The website offers revised templates, videos, and resources to begin or refine your Impact Team journey.)
- You can access more case studies with the QR code in the online appendix

## Book Format:

- We wrote our book for busy educators. It's straightforward. You can swallow it whole, from beginning to end, or read it in chunks based on your needs.
- Chapter 1 introduces the concept of Impact Teams. It is an overview, like reading the back cover of a book—but with a bit more detail.
- Chapters 2 through 8  use the same format
- Chapter 9 invites you to reimagine PLCs

## Chapter Organization:

- A cool quote that pertains to the topic of the chapter
- An appreciative inquiry question that connects your experience to the topic
- The "The *What*" section briefly explains the defined topic.
- The "The *Why*" section outlines why the topic is critical to Impact Team success.
- The "The *How*" section describes the implementation process.
- The "Nutshell" summarizes each chapter.
- Dr. Michael De Sousa wrote the team reflection and equity reflections
- The "Check-In" (a checklist or rubric reflection) allows the prospective Impact Team (PLC) to check their progress and plan the next steps.
- We threaded tips through the chapters, including book suggestions, tools, or processes that may help Impact Team.
- The online appendix contains Impact Team implementation resources for peer facilitators, teachers, leaders, and teams.


With love and gratitude,

Paul and Barb

# Why Reflect on Equity

While there are some exceptional school districts, a handful of stand-out schools, and evidence of incremental progress over time, American public schools have effectively conserved historic disparities in educational access and student achievement. Alone, schools cannot remedy generational, persistent, and systemic inequality. However, effective and equitable schooling can be a flywheel for social mobility, opportunity, and justice.

As we shared in the Introduction, the history of racism and exclusion in public schools are deeply rooted and have caused generational harm to far too many. Working for equity in our schools and classrooms requires us to envision and realize communities and schools where patterns of belonging, access, and achievement are no longer predictive by race, class, language, gender, sexuality, disability, or neurodiversity.

The work of equity starts inward. Committing to equity requires us to reflect inward to unpack our identities, values, and experiences and how they shape our perceptions, decisions, and relationships. It means taking the time to notice, wonder, and act when inequity, exclusion, or harm occurs. Equity requires us to take responsibility for dynamics and patterns of power and relationships that we may not have created—but have the agency to change.

To understand the social, political, and historical context of schooling, we must study equity. Becoming equity-centered educators and leaders requires us to understand the history of systemic oppression and take responsibility for the conditions we create. All students—regardless of identity, status, or background—should sense belonging, build self-efficacy, and ultimately realize their purposes and potential.

The work of equity is collective. This book offers a unique perspective on creating more effective schools and classrooms. We can create more just and effective schools through teaming, collaboration networks, and honoring the assets of all learners. Becoming equity-centered educators requires relationships with colleagues where we can take risks, make mistakes, and work through tension, confusion, or discord. We can no longer avoid conversations about race, identity, power, and inequity. This commitment to equity and racial justice is as vital as ever, as Dr. Kimberlé Williams Crenshaw shared in the following quote.

*"There's been a campaign over the last two years to eliminate our ability to think about race and racism. To talk about race and racism. And, of course, if you can't think or talk about something, guess what? You can't change it."*

At the close of each chapter, we offer *Equity Reflection Questions* so we can practice thinking and talking about these issues. We reflect on these questions to check your assumptions and make our work accessible to and reflective of the people at the center of each (the students, families, and educators). We don't treat these sets of equity reflections as a checklist. Rather, they invite you to pause, reflect, notice, and consider your next steps.

## OVERARCHING REFLECTIONS:

- How do our experiences and identities influence our decisions and how others perceive our leadership?
- What patterns of power and relationships shape any given situation?
- How does our discourse with and about our students, community, and work) affect our thinking, decisions, and practices?
- How can we honor the assets of all our students and avoid focusing on the perceived deficits of students and communities?

- What must we learn or unlearn to lead across the differences that exist between peers, our students, and our community?
- How can we avoid displacing blame for systemic challenges on our students and their families?
- How can we remain committed to, responsible for, and reflective of what's under our control?
- How are we actively countering the impacts of systemic racism, classism, sexism, homophobia, and ableism in our work with students and each other?
- How can we make our classrooms and collaboration safe and inclusive for all students and peers?
- What must we learn about systemic oppression and historical inequity in schools to become stronger leaders for equity in our schools and classrooms?
- What must we understand about our own identities, experiences, values, and perspectives to be more confident and effective leaders for justice?

As you engage with the Impact Teams framework, we encourage you to pause, notice, wonder, and act in new ways. Lean into uncomfortable dialogues and challenges, attend to tension as it arises, and invest in the relationships that will sustain the work. We can expand our impact through intention and care, build beloved communities, and create more equitable schools.

**Dr. Michael De Sousa**

# DEFINING IMPACT TEAMS

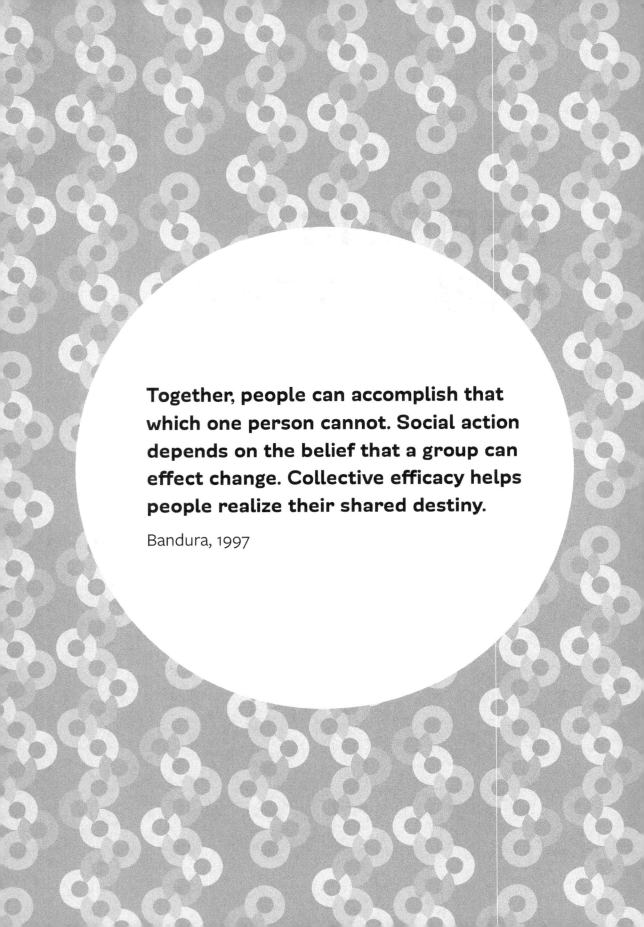

Together, people can accomplish that which one person cannot. Social action depends on the belief that a group can effect change. Collective efficacy helps people realize their shared destiny.

Bandura, 1997

### Self-Empowerment

Our learning network has partnered with over 1500 schools and thousands of teams, driven by the notion of self-empowerment. Self-empowerment means making a conscious decision to take charge of your destiny while making a positive difference in the lives of others.

# THE *WHAT:* TRANSFORM PROFESSIONAL LEARNING COMMUNITIES

How can we center our schools on developing agency for *all* learners? We all want our learners to have agency. We want our learners to develop the knowledge, dispositions, and skills to be critical of global inequities while leveraging their assets to build learning power. We want them to develop their decision-making abilities for informed personal, family, community, and professional choices. Learner agency involves learners actively, purposefully, and constructively directing their own learning growth while contributing positively to the growth of their peers (Calvert, 2016). Bray and McClaskey (2017) describe seven elements that cultivate and develop learner agency: voice, choice, engagement, motivation, ownership, purpose, and self-efficacy. Advancing learner agency is at the heart of the Impact Team Model.

Our goal as educators is to build a culture of efficacy where every learner thrives. We define learners as 'every learner' in our community: students, families, educators, and staff. When we started thinking about refocusing a school's energy on developing the agency of absolutely every learner, we realized that professional learning communities (PLCs) could be the true agents of change. Tapping into existing structures in nearly every school in America, team planning time infused with the Impact Team Model (ITM) would refocus *traditional* PLCs on developing efficacy and agency by combining two existing practices.

1. Formative assessment is a process that happens in the *classroom* and involves students in every aspect of their assessment experience (Stiggins & Chappuis, 2006).

2. Collaborative inquiry, anchored by the tenets of design thinking, allows *teacher teams* to understand their impact on student learning by strengthening their collaborative expertise.

The ITM promotes a school culture where educators, students, and families partner in learning. Through this partnership, the ITM continuously strengthens collective efficacy through collaborative inquiry with the mission of advancing learner agency.

## OUR LEARNERS

As stated earlier, we define learners as all learners in our communities: students, families, educators, and staff. The ITM operationalizes the formative assessment process in the classroom, and across our systems, by relentlessly focusing on the learning process. This model invites and encourages learners to:

- clearly state the goals of learning and the criteria required to progress and achieve mastery in state standards, 21st-century skills, learning habits, social and emotional learning (SEL) competencies, and professional educator standards
- engage in accurate self- and peer assessment to effectively communicate their current learning stage and identify their next learning steps
- understand and articulate their current learning level (surface, deep, or transfer)
- build their capacity to "learn how to learn" (metacognition)
- give and receive accurate, respectful, and descriptive feedback

- develop challenging and possible (*stretch*) learning goals
- revise their work using feedback
- monitor their learning competencies progress and mastery
- celebrate progress via student-led conferences, learning exhibitions, and professional learning celebrations
- contribute positively to the learning of others.

## TEACHER LEARNING TEAMS

Impact Teams (or PLCs) meet frequently to understand their impact on student learning and take collective action—to make a difference for all learners. They come together expressly to learn together in service of and support to all students. The ITM creates a focused structure for teacher teams to engage in collaborative inquiry. Trained peer facilitators guide their colleagues over time. Leadership prioritizes instructional improvement by actively participating in professional learning. This allows teams the autonomy to engage in collaborative inquiry as a vehicle for continuous improvement.

Impact teams can take on many forms: grade-level, course-alike, department or division, vertical, school-level instructional leadership, district leadership, multi-tiered systems of support (MTSS), and equity teams. Regardless of the team's makeup, educators in Impact Teams partner with students, families, and colleagues to advance learner agency. They build and scale their collaborative expertise. They relentlessly pursue understanding their impact on student learning. They ensure that students develop agency and the capacity to make solid decisions for themselves, their families, and their communities.

## 10 PURPOSEFUL PROTOCOLS FOR COLLABORATIVE INQUIRY

Districts often ask teams to engage in collaborative inquiry but are not given the tools and structures to do inquiry effectively. Over the course of the book, you will learn about 10 purposeful protocols to conduct a collaborative inquiry in team meetings and partnering with students. Each Impact Team protocol uses a three-phase Evidence–Analysis–Action (EAA) framework. As teams become familiar with the framework, they realize they can use it to analyze and triangulate evidence sources, including student voice, universal screener, climate, observational, family perception data, and student work. See Figure 1.1 for clarity of the EAA framework.

**Figure 1.1 EAA framework**

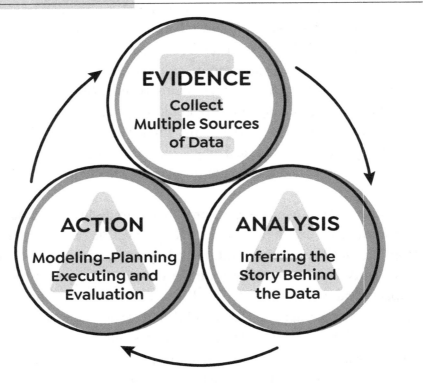

Use the 10 Impact Team protocols to anchor each PLC meeting. They refine and support the "assessment for learning experiences" with students in the classroom, ensuring a knowledge-sharing and building focus. We aligned our inquiry process to the tenets of design thinking, ensuring teams adopt a solution-focused approach to advancing learner agency. We describe our collaborative inquiry framework more in Chapter 4, Teaming to Learn.

## TRANSFORM THE FOUR PLC QUESTIONS

ITM centers on the learning process, setting it apart from other PLC models. Rachel Carrillo Fairchild, author and Impact Team coach, helped our other coaches with this shift. She re-envisioned the PLC questions from the perspective of the learner. Remember: we define learners as everyone in a system: students, educators, support staff, and families. This means holding everyone accountable for using multiple evidence sources when justifying their answers to the following questions.

**Evidence:**
**What do I expect to learn?**

- Learning intentions and success criteria
- Executive functioning and self-regulation
- Social and emotional learning competencies
- Metacognition

**Analysis:**
**How will I know I am learning?**

- Feedback, self and peer assessment, reflection, and metacognition:
  □ Where am I going? Relevance?
  □ Where am I now?
  □ What is my next learning step?

**Action:**
**How will I adjust my learning?**

- Revision and deliberate practice
- Collaboration
- More feedback

**Action:**
**What will I do if I already know it?**

- Contribute to others
- Apply learning to new contexts
- Accelerate my learning

We transformed the four PLC questions into learner-centered questions and aligned them to the EAA framework (Evidence–Analysis–Action). The four PLC questions focus on teachers, while the ITM inquiry questions center on learners and their assets.

## IMPACT TEAMS ARE DIFFERENT

When understanding how this model differs from other school transformation models, it may be easier to discuss how it does not.

The ITM is not

- solely focused on analyzing benchmarks, common formative assessments (CFAs), and summative assessment data with little time to respond to student needs;
- a method to sort students into ability tracks
- a team that solely fills in a complicated template for the principal
- teachers that only meet for compliance and accountability
- teams that use an agenda determined by site leadership.

Table 1.1 explains how this model may differ from more traditional PLC practices in schools.

**Table 1.1 PLCs vs. Impact Teams**

| | Similarities | Differences |
|---|---|---|
| **Purpose** | • Increasing student achievement<br>• Improving instructional practices | • Purposefully strengthens student, teacher, and collective efficacy<br>• Advances learner and teacher agency through inquiry<br>• Attends to identity, power, and relationships<br>• Implements formative assessment ("assessment for learning") into the classroom<br>• Focuses on progress and healthy learning identities in stakeholders, honoring their assets and funds of knowledge<br>• Directs focus on what's working well—and building on that success<br>• Responds to feedback (evidence) with collective actions anchored by research |

|  | Similarities | Differences |
|---|---|---|
| **Processes** | • The 4 PLC questions drive the inquiry<br>• Sharing ideas around effective practice<br>• Norming effective collaboration | • Uses four learner-centered inquiry questions.<br>• Adopts human-centered design/design thinking to ground the collaborative inquiry process.<br>• Employs Universal three-phase (EAA) protocol framework (Evidence Analysis Action) at all organizational levels<br>• Emphasizes collaborative inquiry using 10 purposeful protocols in and outside the classroom, anchored by the EAA framework.<br>• Stems from appreciative inquiry and asset-based pedagogies. |
| **Instruction** | • Using best practices to guide instruction | • Emphasizes self-regulation and metacognition (using the Visible Learning high-impact influences)<br>• Advances asset-based pedagogies, including culturally responsive and sustaining educational practices<br>• Adopts a formative mindset by using learning intentions, success criteria, peer and self-assessment, reflection, questioning, feedback, and goal setting<br>• Plans for all levels of rigor (surface, deep, and transfer)<br>• Exchanges grading for high-quality, multiple-source feedback |

|  | Similarities | Differences |
|---|---|---|
| **Structure** | • Recursively cycles collaborative teacher inquiry or action research<br>• Job-alike teams<br>• Shared or distributed leadership | • Bases team configurations on the purpose<br>• Develops and supports collaborative leadership within the team—and across the school |
| **Evidence Sources** | • Analysis of CFAs, universal screeners, and benchmark assessments | • Triangulation of multiple sources of evidence (qualitative and quantitative): student work, student voice, and school climate, SEL, and screening data<br>• emphasizes current student work analysis<br>• Understands the true story behind the data<br>• Bases assessment tasks on criteria<br>• Assessment tasks are designed at all levels of rigor (surface, deep, and transfer) |

## Personal Reflection:

Based on what you have learned so far, how is the ITM different from the current PLC practices you use? What do you appreciate about the differences?

# THE *WHY*: THE POWER OF EFFICACY

## OUR EDUCATIONAL LANDSCAPE

With the enactment of the No Child Left Behind legislation (2002), focus shifted from an emphasis on learning to standardized test achievement. Superficially, this emphasis did not appear to be very different from previous eras of "school reform." However, over the last decade we have seen that achievement and learning are not synonymous. Simply put, achievement is the arm of accountability, while learning is the life skill. With accountability as an unyielding force, we often compromise learning. Unfortunately, the drive to raise test scores often victimizes students and teachers.

An unrelenting focus on absolute achievement significantly impacts the culture of many of our schools. It directly and negatively impacts teachers' sense of efficacy, collectively and individually (Finnigan & Daly, 2013). Admittedly, the stakes are high for our teachers, leaders, and schools. The drive for achievement regarding high-stakes testing is understandable. However, along the way, we often sacrifice the notion of 'learning' in our quest for "all students will be proficient or above."

Thankfully, the winds shifted with December 2015's Every Student Succeeds Act (ESSA) legislation, which takes a more balanced approach to accountability. However, changing practices grounded in annual test results—and implemented for over a decade—will take time. This shift and the devastating impact of the pandemic created chaos in many of our nation's schools. Longstanding school inequities became even more visible, and opportunity gaps continued to widen. We designed the ITM for schools to use as a framework to move from summative tests to using formative assessments to monitor. This allows us to support student growth and respond to diverse learning needs.

Beware another initiative? Or is this a way to repurpose existing practices to have a greater impact? We work in all sizes, sorts, and flavors of schools. We are currently partnering with over 500 schools nationwide, from remote to rural to urban to suburban. We know from experience that in our current educational landscape, when educators hear the words *reform* or *assessment*, they think it means *more testing*. When they think "test," they think or say the following:

- I will be judged or evaluated by this.
- It takes away from my teaching time.
- It takes too long to grade.
- Many children need the schema or stamina to do well on tests.
- This will shut down struggling kids.

However, Impact Teams value the formative assessment process, which involves and honors students in every aspect of the assessment experience. This is a strengths-based model that focuses on teacher teams discovering what works well in their school. It builds upon existing strengths and students' assets. Our intention is not to fix broken students, teachers, or systems. We intend to support schools by creating conditions where innovation and creativity thrive. "When people focus on human ideals and achievements, peak experiences, and best practices, these things—not the conflicts—tend to flourish" (Mohr & Watkins, 2002).

We must always remember that our core business *is* learning, not dispensing information, not raising test scores, not clever pedagogy, not technology tools. And "the learning" concerns not just students but our entire community. We must relentlessly learn together to ensure student progress. At its best, learning together results in a pervasive attitude of "We can do this!" School cultures committed to learning together are schools in which efficacy thrives. Restoring the belief that teachers as a group can—and do—make a difference is the impetus of our model.

## THE RESEARCH

In 2009, John Hattie published a seminal meta-analytic synthesis, *Visible Learning*. It has been periodically updated to include additional studies. Since a .40 effect size (ES) represents approximately one year of growth in one year, education leaders and teachers must focus on factors that guarantee *at least* a year's prog-

When people focus on human ideals and achievements, peak experiences, and best practices, these things—not the conflicts—tend to flourish (Mohr & Watkins, 2002).

ress for all students (.40 or above). Developing and designing ITM reflects extensive research on practices that maximize student learning. Many of these practices emphasize self-regulation and metacognition. Impact Teams put into practice several factors proven to have the greatest impact on student learning. The following sample demonstrates several high-impact influences. According to the Visible Learning MetaX database, researchers updated these effect sizes in June 2023.

| **Student Learning Strategies With Effect Size (ES)** | | |
|---|---|---|
| | Self-judgment/reflection | .85 |
| | Meta-cognitive strategies | .59 |
| | Self-regulation strategies | .54 |
| | Strategy monitoring | .58 |
| | Transfer strategies | .86 |
| | Peer tutoring | .47 |
| | Deliberate practice | .79 |
| | Summarizing | .70 |
| | Assessment capable | 1.02 |
| **Teaching Strategies With Effect Size (ES)** | Clear goal intentions | .51 |
| | Success criteria | .88 |
| | Peer and self-grading | .54 |
| | Goal commitment | .40 |
| | Feedback tasks–process | .65 |
| | Feedback timing | .82 |
| | Questioning | .51 |
| | Response to intervention | .74 |
| | Reciprocal teaching | .74 |
| | Scaffolding | .60 |
| **Teacher and School With Effect Size (ES)** | Teacher expectations | .44 |
| | Relationships with students | .47 |
| | Teacher clarity | .84 |
| | Estimates of achievement | 1.21 |
| | Microteaching | .90 |
| | School climate | .49 |
| | Collective teacher efficacy | 1.36 |

## Team Reflection:

☐ How do you learn about your students' and families' assets? How does your team ensure that students have agency over learning?

☐ What can teams do to put learners into the driver's seat?

☐ How can you ensure teams amplify the Visible Learning strategies most effectively?

## Equity Reflection:

☐ How can we develop our ability to critically analyze inequity?

☐ What does our team believe and understand about equity and systemic oppression?

☐ What do we need to learn—or unlearn—together?

# THE POWER OF EFFICACY

Academic progress in a school is not only a reflection of the sum of the individual contributions but also the collective whole: how teachers work together (Bandura 1994, 1997). A collective sense of efficacy in a school community contributes significantly to academic achievement (Bandura 2000). It was a *more powerful predictor than socioeconomic status* and as powerful as prior academic achievement. This does not mean that collective teacher efficacy can solve the longstanding opportunity gaps plaguing our nation's citizens. We must relentlessly dismantle the systemic barriers that harm our shared humanity. However, this profound research illustrates the power of our shared beliefs when helping our students reach their full potential.

# THE *HOW*: THE STEPS TO SUCCESS

We designed this book for instructional leadership teams, instructional leaders, and teacher teams who want to expand their collaborative formative assessment practices. Each chapter clearly defines the success criteria for successful implementation with chapter check-Ins.

## THE STEPS TO SUCCESS

- Chapter 2: Build a Culture of Efficacy
  - » What: The four sources of efficacy
  - » Why: Impact on student learning
  - » How: Planning for efficacy

- Chapter 3: Cultivate a Teaming Culture
  - » What: Teaming cultures
  - » Why: Building quality connections
  - » How: Developing agreements and core values

- Chapter 4: Teaming to Learn
  - » What: Collaborative inquiry
  - » Why: Building collective efficacy
  - » How: Architecting the Impact Team Model

- Chapter 5: Strengthen Student Efficacy: The Formative Assessment Process in Action
  - » What: Assessment for learning
  - » Why: Building student efficacy
  - » How: Purposeful protocols to strengthen assessment for learning

- Chapter 6: Create Conditions for Efficacy: Ensure an Equitable-Viable-Coherent Curriculum
  - » What: Quality curriculum
  - » Why: Student clarity and strengthening efficacy
  - » How: Steps for success

- Chapter 7: Evidence to Inform and Act
  - » What: Using quality evidence to inform and act
  - » Why: Springboard for action
  - » How: Purposeful protocols for data use

- Chapter 8: Activate a Guiding Coalition
  - » What: A guiding coalition
  - » Why: Growing capacity from within
  - » How: Forming and sustaining an Impact Team coalition

- Chapter 9: Our Invitation to You

- Digital Appendix

# BUILDING
# A CULTURE
# OF EFFICACY

**As teachers in a school feel empowered to do great things, great things happen.**

Eells, 2011, p. 4

## Mastery Moment

Think of an experience when you felt such confidence and optimism that you believed anything was possible. Why was that belief so strong? What conditions created those powerful feelings?

# THE *WHAT:* THE FOUR SOURCES OF EFFICACY

Efficacy is a concept that is often misunderstood. It feels like it should connect to effectiveness and efficiency. And it does—sort of. *Efficacy* is the ability to produce a desired or intended effect. It is about the *belief* in the ability to effect change. Imagine a school where efficacy is pervasive, where teachers and students alike believe in their capacity to learn despite challenges, and where a growth mindset prevails—a culture of efficacy.

Taken a step further, collective efficacy is more than collaboration, more than a teacher team talking every Wednesday afternoon. Over time, collaborating effectively towards collective goals, through thick and thin, fosters collective efficacy. Collaboration results in the group's collective *belief* in their power to effect positive change. It includes knowledge building through learning from one another. It involves the optimism, confidence, and resiliency that evolves from successful teacher and student learning experiences.

Impact Teams, a network of educators who partner with students and each other in learning, develop and nurture efficacy. These teams commit to understanding their impact on learning. The stronger their beliefs about their collective capabilities, the more they achieve. Impact Teams empower learners to own and take charge of their learning. Ultimately, they build a culture of efficacy.

# UNDERSTANDING SELF-EFFICACY

To understand collective teacher efficacy, one must understand self-efficacy: one's confidence in their ability to achieve a goal or outcome (Bandura, 1997). It is what we all strive for, both personally and professionally. The human drive to be efficacious has resulted in a multi-billion-dollar industry around self-actualization, health and fitness, business, and all sorts of purported pathways to personal success.

Ultimately, however, self-efficacy is a belief in the ability to succeed. Not surprisingly, self-efficacy significantly relates to success and highly correlates with confidence and optimism.

## Four Sources of Self-Efficacy

Efficacy sounds and feels like something we all want in spades. It is a quality we want all our students to develop. What does it take to develop efficacy? Four major sources contribute to developing self-efficacy beliefs (Bandura, 1977; A. W. Hoy, 2000).

- *Mastery Experiences*: Successful experiences influence your perspective about your abilities. These experiences boost self-efficacy. Mastery experiences are the most robust source. In this text, we call these mastery experiences *mastery moments.*
- *Vicarious Experiences*: We define these *success models* that serve as an integral source of self-efficacy. Observing someone else perform a task or handle a situation effectively can help you to perform the same task by imitation. We learn vicariously through others; they are efficacy mentors.
- *Social and Verbal Persuasion*: We loosely define these as *feedback*. Credible communication and descriptive feedback can boost self-efficacy, guiding and motivating learners to successfully complete a task.
- *Positive Emotional State*: We interpret this state as *safety*. A learner must feel safe. Security creates a positive emotional state and a willingness to take risks and embrace mistakes as learning opportunities. For this reason, school climate impacts self-efficacy.

 **Tip 2.1**: Believing in yourself helps you achieve what you set out to do, and results in a healthier, more effective, and generally more successful life. Albert Bandura articulates his self-efficacy theory in the book *Self Efficacy: The Exercise of Control.*

## Student Self-Efficacy

Student self-efficacy takes center stage in the much-researched area of motivation. In the context of schools, it is a belief in one's capabilities to learn and achieve intended learning intentions. In a classroom, you can see student self-efficacy as a strong "I can" attitude. In contrast, a student with low self-efficacy tends to believe "I can't" when given a learning task. The negative perception is often academic-content specific, such as "I'm not a good writer" or "I'm not good at math."

Students with strong self-efficacy

- motivate themselves intrinsically and put forth a high degree of effort
- challenge themselves with difficult tasks
- persistently problem-solve to "get unstuck"
- resiliently see mistakes as learning opportunities
- confidently achieve personal goals.

Students are not born with self-efficacy. They acquire it in the same way adults build it, through the following experiences adapted from Bandura (1977) and Hoy (2000).

- mastery moments
- success models (learning vicariously through others),
- feedback (verbal persuasion)
- safety

Fortunately, formative assessment inherently encompasses these four sources of self-efficacy. They integrally work as a component of the Impact Team Model. Specific teaching strategies, such as cooperative learning, student goal setting, revision, and peer and self-assessment, also strengthen self-efficacy (Fencl & Scheel, 2005).

These methods put students in the driver's seat. To ensure safety, fostering an equitable, positive culture is key. Transformative social and emotional learning (SEL) instruction contributes to developing efficacy, as well as the adoption of restorative practices. (Restorative practices focus on strengthening relationships for both youth and adults in a school community.) Developing self-efficacy is built into the processes of a learner-centered classroom where metacognition and self-regulation are taught, modeled, and expected.

## Self-Efficacy and Learning Identity

Self-efficacy relates to learner identity (how we perceive ourselves as learners). People with healthy learning identities view and understand themselves as learners. Mastery experiences realized through productive struggles develop healthy learning identities. A person develops core learning habits when they make mistakes—and get back up and try again.

We learn perseverance skills by actively navigating challenges. We learn to problem solve by solving problems. And we learn to make decisions by being *allowed* to make them, even when we encounter setbacks. One's cultural identity shapes a person's learner identity. We make meaning and understand the world through our lived experiences: vital sources of knowledge that we can build new knowledge. Anchoring our teaching practices in asset-based pedagogies allows learners to build upon the gifts they already have. That allows them to build their self-efficacy and, in turn, assists with developing healthy learning identities.

**Tip 2.2**: Check out chapter three in *Amplify Learner Voice through Culturally Responsive Assessment*. The authors recommend one-on-one interviews, focus groups, and engaging students in reflection about how they perceive themselves as learners.

## Teacher Self-Efficacy

*Teacher self-efficacy refers to* the teacher's confidence in their ability to promote student learning (A. W. Hoy, 2000), a concept first discussed over 35 years ago.

A teacher's self-efficacy ties to their perception of their capabilities in fostering students' learning and engagement. A teacher's belief in their ability to promote positive change for students has proven to have a positive influence on student achievement, motivation (Moolenaar et al., 2011), and positive attitudes toward school (Miskel et al., 1983). This confidence and optimism lead to perseverance and a commitment to reaching—and often exceeding—learning goals.

A teacher's confidence level in their ability to promote learning can depend on past experiences and school cultures. Considering the research findings, Jerald (2007) highlights teacher behaviors that often relate to teachers' sense of efficacy.

Teachers with a strong sense of efficacy tend to

- exhibit greater levels of planning and organization,
- remain open to new ideas and willingly experiment with new methods
- resiliently persistent when things do not go smoothly
- act less critical of student errors
- refer difficult students to special education less often.

In an interview with Anita Woolfolk, a researcher in the field of teacher efficacy, Woolfolk and Shaughnessy (2004) describe the practical implications of the research.

> *Teachers who set goals, persist, and try another strategy when one approach is found wanting—in other words, teachers who have a high sense of efficacy and act on it—are more likely to have students who learn. (pp. 156–157)*

## Collective Teacher Efficacy

Rooted in self-efficacy, collective efficacy means a group's shared beliefs about their collective capability to promote successful student outcomes (Goddard et al., 2000). Collective efficacy involves more than positive thinking. It ultimately ties to collective

Teachers who set goals, persist, and try another strategy when one approach is found wanting—in other words, teachers who have a high sense of efficacy and act on it—are more likely to have students who learn.

Woolfolk and Shaughnessy, 2004, pp. 156–157

action: the ability to make things happen. We define this ability as "agency."

Building a strong school culture requires a system-wide focus on strengthening student and teacher self-efficacy. Eells (2011) defines collective teacher efficacy as the pervasive belief that directly affects the school's ability to increase achievement. Jenni Donohoo (2017) describes six enabling conditions for fostering collective teacher efficacy:

(1) advance teacher influence

(2) goal consensus

(3) knowledge about one another's work

(4) cohesive staff

(5) responsiveness of leadership

(6) effective systems of intervention.

We must nurture and develop collective teacher efficacy. A belief in all learners in the system (families, students, educators, and staff) lies at the heart of the Impact Team Model.

 **Tip 2.3**: To read more about the six enabling conditions that foster collective efficacy, check out Jenni Donohoo's book, *Collective Efficacy: How Educators' Beliefs Impact Student Learning*.

## Personal Reflection:

How much time does your school devote to developing and nurturing the six conditions that foster collective teacher efficacy?

# THE *WHY:* RESEARCH AND REASONS

Strengthening efficacy at all levels of the school dramatically improves student learning. If teachers and students feel powerful, they can surmount obstacles, persist when challenged, and expend the necessary effort to learn. We have highlighted the following four reasons.

## REASON 1: EFFICACY HAS THE GREATEST INFLUENCE ON STUDENT LEARNING.

John Hattie (2023) identified *collective teacher efficacy* (CTE) as the single most powerful influence on student achievement. With an effect size of 1.36, collective teacher efficacy nearly quadruples the rate of student learning (Eells, 2011). In fact, W. K. Hoy and colleagues (2002) found that collective teacher efficacy has a *greater influence on student achievement than socioeconomic status.* (An influence with a .40 effect size is equal to about 1 year's growth in 1 year.) CTE cannot solve the longstanding "opportunity gaps" that plague our nation's systems. But *it does* mean that our shared beliefs and values about teaching and learning improve people's lives.

## REASON 2: EFFICACY CREATES AND SUSTAINS A LEARNING CULTURE.

When schools intentionally plan for the four sources of efficacy, they effectively build knowledge together. Knowledge building and sharing thrive in a learning culture. Teachers and students not only learn at an accelerated rate, but they also learn *how* to learn, self-regulate, persevere, communicate, and problem-solve.

## REASON 3: CREATING THE CONDITIONS FOR EFFICACY FOCUSES ON A SYSTEM'S STRENGTHS.

When schools aim to ensure mastery experiences, they focus on building off people's strengths instead of identifying deficits. The studies on positive imagery suggest that employees who hold self-images of competence and success are likelier to achieve high-performance levels than those with poor self-esteem (Mohr & Watkins, 2002).

## REASON 4: EFFICACY CREATES A HEALTHY CLIMATE.

Learning accelerates when people feel safe. Having a learning community that believes it can accomplish great things is vital for the health of a school (Eells, 2011). Imagine a school where making mistakes is understood as part of the learning process. Imagine a school where students and teachers embrace risks and seek learning opportunities. A sense of belonging in school may impact a young person's well-being and educational trajectory (Waters et al., 2010).

# THE *HOW:* PLANNING FOR EFFICACY

You hold the power to build a culture of efficacy! But you have to intentionally plan for it. The four sources of efficacy, illustrated in Figure 2.1., lie as the foundation for developing self- and collective efficacy.

**Figure 2.1: Four Sources of Efficacy**

Leadership teams purposely and thoughtfully develop a plan for multiple and ongoing opportunities to experience the four sources of efficacy when building a schoolwide culture.

## 1.   MASTERY MOMENTS:

To build confidence, teams need to experience success through mastery. Teacher teams need direct experience that they interpret as successful. These successes increase confidence and build resiliency. Interestingly, the research clarifies that "easy success" does not contribute to a sense of collective efficacy. Quick and easy success, followed by failure, produces discouragement (Goddard et al., 2000). However, when teams take on challenging goals and overcome obstacles, they come away with a robust belief in their collective efficacy.

## 2.   MODELS OF SUCCESS:

Learning vicariously through others' successes also builds efficacy. Observing successful practices of other teams and/or schools provides indirect experiences that translate into doable practice.

Think of it as a source of modeling effective practice. Groups that observe other successful teams can view themselves as capable of similar performances.

## 3.   FEEDBACK:

We know that feedback doubles the learning rate—and that's not just for students. We learn through descriptive and timely feedback. Teams that collectively focus on improvement commit to research, take risks, share knowledge and skills, and use feedback to learn from one another. But not all feedback is created equally, and not all feedback is heard. A key ingredient to effective teams is diving deeply into productive feedback practices. "Feedback from multiple sources, including their teachers, can broaden and deepen learners' reflection and lead to an effective revision of their understanding, products, and performances." (Bloomberg, et al., 2022, p. 327) It positively, appreciatively, and productively moves groups forward. Success becomes possible with forward movement—and it comes from increasing collective efficacy.

## 4.   SAFETY:

A sustainable, positive school climate fosters healthy learning identities by honoring the dignity of each person's cultural identity. This aspect is necessary for a productive, contributing, and satisfying life in a democratic society. School climate includes collective agreements, shared values, and positive expectations that support people feeling socially, emotionally and physically safe. Relational trust builds effective teams, translating into team members who genuinely listen to one another, respect differing opinions, and willingly share knowledge. Everyone feels accepted, respected, and empowered by their teammates. To build trust, teams must first take their "trust temperature." You can find several trust surveys online (e.g., Tschannen-Moran et al., 1998). Use baseline trust level data, then commit to collaborative ways to build trust around weak points. Check the trust temp every 3 to 4 months to ensure a continued commitment to a safe team environment.

> **When teacher teams believe they can make a positive impact with all students, even the ones who may be hard to reach, they have collective efficacy.**

## NUTSHELL

We planted the roots of efficacy at the student, teacher, and collective levels in the previous pages. And while student and teacher efficacy correlates with improved achievement, *collective* teacher efficacy accelerates learning even more. Quite simply, sharing knowledge and developing skills reaps significant gains. Improving student achievement system-wide crucially raises the collective efficacy beliefs of the staff (Goddard et al. 2000). Believing in the combined intellect, shared commitment, and focused energy of a group accelerates an even greater learning impact.

When teacher teams believe they can make a positive impact with all students, even the ones who may be hard to reach, they have collective efficacy. The explicitly designed Impact Team Model builds teacher, student, and collective efficacy: the pervasive belief that directly affects the school's ability to increase achievement (Eells, 2011).

## Team Reflection:

List some ways the leadership team provides opportunities to:

☐ experience mastery moments or mastery experiences
☐ share successful models and learn vicariously
☐ learn to effectively give and receive descriptive feedback
☐ build consensus through shared decision-making
☐ possess the autonomy to determine the PLC learning focus
☐ create a safe team and school environment

## Equity Reflection:

☐ How can we define self-efficacy in a culturally sustaining manner?
☐ How can we contextualize collective and self-efficacy within equity goals?
☐ What patterns do we notice?
☐ How can we dismantle the predictability of self-efficacy?
☐ Do all students have access to identity-affirming success models?

# CHECK-IN

Use the rubric below with your team to analyze your current learning community climate. Add ideas and next steps to maximize your collaborative expertise during this reflection.

| School Climate | Not Yet | Sometimes | Often |
|---|---|---|---|
| We co-construct SEL and behavioral intentions with students. | | | |
| We use proactive practices related to social and emotional learning. | | | |
| Our community implements practices so all learners take responsibility for their actions to repair harm. | | | |
| Our community identifies and implements practices so all demographic and identity groups feel affirmed, validated, and accepted. | | | |
| What's next? | | | |
| Strengthening Efficacy | Not Yet | Sometimes | Often |
| Our school intentionally plans for ways to strengthen stakeholder trust, belonging, and efficacy. | | | |
| Our school analyzes evidence regarding relational trust, belonging, and efficacy to strengthen learner agency. | | | |

| Strengthening Efficacy, continued | Not Yet | Sometimes | Often |
|---|---|---|---|
| Leadership demonstrates vulnerability to strengthen relational trust. | | | |
| Our school values diverse ideas when solving practice puzzles. | | | |
| Educators know one another's strengths. | | | |
| Our school community co-constructs shared values, agreements, and school goals through shared decision-making with all stakeholders. | | | |
| Our community uses asset-based approaches to build a strong learning culture. | | | |
| Adults and students model core learning habits that cultivate healthy identities in our stakeholders. | | | |
| What's next? | | | |

# Reflection Activity:

During a PLC or Impact Team Meeting, each member determines where your team lies on the CTE continuum. Everyone shares their thoughts before building consensus and setting efficacy goals.

| Collective Teacher Efficacy Continuum | |
|---|---|
| Low CTE ◄——————————————  ——————————————► High CTE | |
| **Pervasive doubt:** Feel powerless over circumstances beyond their control and expect undesirable results (a deficit mindset). | **Optimistic:** Share the belief that all students can achieve at least 1 year's growth in 1 year (a growth mindset). |
| **Uncertainty:** Doubt that they can teach or reach certain students. | **Confidence:** Believe they can effectively teach every student. |
| **Isolated:** Feel alone in their specific responsibilities and challenges and express doubts about the team/group. | **Collaborative:** Believe in the power of collective thought through goal consensus. |
| **Know enough:** See themselves as experts who know enough to deliver what "needs to be taught." | **Learners all:** See themselves as learners, value errors, seek feedback, and learn from one another. |
| **Apathy:** Feel powerless and put in minimum effort. | **Perseverance:** Possess staying power based on a commitment to success and believe in the power of their interventions. |

# Reflection Activity:

Purposefully plan for efficacy. Use this organizer to develop a plan for strengthening efficacy with your instructional leadership team. Fold a piece of chart paper into fourths. Label each box accordingly. List and describe specific ways your team can strengthen stakeholder self-efficacy.

| Mastery Moments | Model of Success |
|---|---|
| *Example: Teachers record video examples of effective practice.* | *Example: Teachers watch effective teaching videos and discuss what made the practice effective.* |
| **Feedback** | **Safety** |
| *Example: Noting strengths, the principal gives positive feedback regarding school focus practices during evidence walks.* | *Example: The staff takes a relational trust survey and discusses the results and action steps three times during the year.* |

# CULTIVATING A TEAMING CULTURE

**[Trust] is earned not through heroic deeds, or even highly visible actions, but through paying attention, listening, and gestures of genuine care and connection.**

Brené Brown, 2018

**Mastery Moment:**

Think of a time you were part of an effective team. What conditions were in place? How can your team nurture similar experiences?

# THE *WHAT*: CULTIVATING A TEAMING CULTURE

Professional collaboration is the activity of learning together to generate new ideas, solve problems, and collectively improve practice. Through continuous improvement, teams begin to see positive impact. When one member focuses on the assets they bring to the team, their peers' assets, and their students' and families' assets, they honor and value the rich funds of knowledge that absolutely everyone brings to the table.

Teachers feel varying levels of self-efficacy regarding their craft. When they collaborate with other teachers with high levels of self-efficacy, they tend to develop higher efficacy beliefs (Siciliano, 2016). Effective collaboration is essential in building a culture of efficacy. However, learning together is easier said than done. Here's the reality: Almost 90% of teachers are part of a team. Most teachers spend less than 1 hour per week formally collaborating with colleagues. Given the 40 hours a week we work in school (not counting the many hours outside of school when we prepare, worry, and plan), that's about 2.5%.

So, how can we make the time spent with colleagues so valuable that they can't wait to get to their meetings to share, learn, debate, and celebrate? How can we make time together productive so we focus more energy on the influences that have the most potential to make a positive impact on learning while building collective expertise. After all, isn't that why we collaborate?

Google conducted a 3-year study on teaming called Project Aristotle (Graham, 2016). Not surprisingly, they found that working effectively together can reap powerful results—that deep and innovative thinking comes from interactive problem-solving. Most businesses now work in teams. Isolation and autonomy are out. Teaming and collaboration are in! Simply put, "We is smarter than me."

Working with schools nationwide and at all levels, learning from missteps and mistakes, we developed a collaborative model that operationalizes what makes teams highly effective, remarkably focused, and capable of strengthening collective efficacy.

 **Tip 3.1**: Read more about Google's Project Oxygen study.

# THE *WHY*: RESEARCH AND REASONS

Developing collective capacity through effective teaming improves schools. Michael Fullan (2010) confirms this assertion: "Collective capacity generates emotional commitment and the technical expertise that no amount of individual capacity working alone can come close to matching." Educators, students, and families can no longer learn in isolation. To meet current and diverse demands, they must learn to learn together. Although there are many reasons why it is important to team up, we highlight three.

# REASON 1: IMPACT TEAMS STRENGTHEN THE CULTURE OF LEARNING.

The Impact Team Model (ITM) creates conditions for a learning culture to exist. Gruenert and Whitaker (2015) describe six types of learning cultures:

1.  Collaborative—embraces learning for all students and adults; feedback flourishes

2.  Comfortable–Collaborative—polite to the point of inhibiting constructive feedback

3.  Contrived–Collegial—leadership determines how the faculty behaves

4.  Balkanized—encourages small-group competition

5.  Fragmented—everyone does their own thing

6.  Toxic—negativity pervades

In the hundreds of schools we have worked with, we have found that most schools view themselves as collaborative. Upon closer examination, many operate with a "contrived-collegial" culture: admin scheduling teachers to complete assigned tasks that match their operating systems and beliefs. Grade-level or course-alike meetings become a to-do list of action items born from a hierarchy. Accountability, rather than learning, drives the bus.

In contrast, the ITM focuses on a networked learning culture that:
   · Shares and develops knowledge formally and informally
   · Builds on the existing strengths of educators, students, families, and community
   · Creates transparent, reciprocal communication pathways where feedback and coaching flourishes
   · Breaks down traditional power structures in exchange for quality learning partnerships
   · Ensures restorative leadership, building quality connections

through identifying and repairing harm
· Learns vicariously through success models
· Creates mastery moment opportunities for all stakeholders

## REASON 2: RELATIONSHIPS AND CONNECTION MATTER.

Leana (2011) of the University of Pittsburgh talks about teacher collaboration in terms of human capital and social capital. Human capital develops the individual teacher in subject area expertise and pedagogical skills. Social capital focuses on developing relationships. It's not just about what the teacher knows but how they gain that knowledge. Leana's study showed that social capital multiplies human capital. Strong student achievement gains result in mastery moments when teachers frequently converse with colleagues about teaching and learning, as well as feeling connection and trust (Bryk & Schneider, 2003).

## REASON 3: TEACHER TEAMS MAKE A POSITIVE IMPACT.

Teachers get better together. Schools that engage in better-quality collaboration have greater achievement gains in math and reading (Ronfeldt et al., 2015). Vanderbilt associate professor, Jason Grissom said, "Focusing on building teacher teams and providing meaningful ways for teachers to work together on the tough challenges they encounter can lead to substantively important achievement gains" (Ronfeldt et al., 2015). In fact, teacher quality improves at greater rates when they work in schools with better-quality collaboration (Ronfeldt et al., 2015). We believe schools have misunderstood achievement gaps, so we use the term "opportunity gap." However, the result of an achievement gap or opportunity gap is the same: students and families are harmed.

# THE *HOW:* THE LEARNING NETWORK

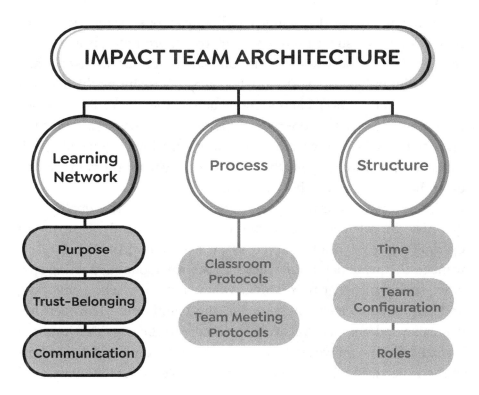

For high-performing teams to realize their collective potential, they need architecture. Impact Teams use a specific infrastructure to do the work. The brick-and-mortar organizational structures and processes of the ITM includes three elements.

- **The learning network**
- The process
- The structure

In this chapter, we focus on the health of your learning organization—your network. A learning network comprises formal and informal relationships where people share and grow knowledge. Our mentor and friend, Dr. Alan Daly, a global researcher in social network theory and organizational change, describes two systems at work in any organization, one "formal" and the other "informal."

A formal network includes individuals possessing positional power, such as a superintendent, director, coordinator, principal, or teacher. Formal network interactions stem from an industrial and typical hierarchical structure (Daly, 2010). These hierarchical structures dominate schools and systems across the globe. There is one person at the top who operates a hierarchy. Knowledge, expertise, and feedback flow downward to others with lower "formal" positions. This hierarchy typically creates an us-versus-them mentality, even though we are on the same team.

In contrast, informal social networks include the quality and quantity of relationships someone possesses (Daly, 2010). For example, when I (Paul) served as an assistant principal, I rarely went to the principal or counselor for advice about supporting specific students. I went to Yolanda. Yolanda was a teacher, advocate, and biliteracy activist integrated in the community. I needed her expertise and perspective since I was new to the organization. In a formal system, you would follow the chain of command, regardless of the expertise and perspective of the people in the hierarchy.

 **Tip 3.2**: In Video 3.1, Dr. Alan Daly describes the power and explains the importance of social networks in educational change.

Quality relationships and strong connections shape school improvement efforts. People in informal systems exchange knowledge, resources, and expertise (Daly, 2010). We aim to grow collaborative expertise from within by harnessing the rich funds of knowledge already in a system through formal and informal learning networks.

## Personal Reflection:

☐ Who are you connected to informally?

    ☐ What is the quality of your informal connections?

    ☐ How can you share and grow knowledge with your informal social network?

☐ Who are you connected to formally?

    ☐ What is the quality of your formal connections?

☐ What would happen if both social networks could share and grow together?

# OUR LEARNING NETWORK

Social networks shape school change. Formal and informal social networks constitute an organization's learning network. Effective collaboration depends on the health of your learning organization's social network. All social networks establish and grow a "teaming to learn" culture. Three foundational components cultivate a learning culture that centralizes human assets.

1. Purpose

2. Relational Trust

3. Communication

# PURPOSE

Devote time to identifying and solidifying the moral purpose of "teaming" and the underlying values of the members. A team shares a common purpose. The ultimate purpose of Impact Teams is strengthening teacher, student, and collective teacher efficacy. With purpose comes commitment, and that commitment synergistically moves things forward.

Discussing and building consensus regarding shared core beliefs underpins the purpose. Beliefs powerfully predict behavior. Carol Dweck (2006) identifies two types of beliefs (or, in her words, mindsets)—growth and fixed. John Hattie (2012) calls these beliefs mindframes. He describes them as "ways of thinking" that drive practices. Use several of Hattie's mindframes for a deep Impact Teams implementation.

- We evaluate the effect of our teaching on student learning.
- We talk more about learning than teaching.
- We are change agents and collaborators.
- We view assessment as feedback.

During the final phase of the pandemic, stakeholders from The Core Collaborative Learning Network convened to co-construct our core values with friend and colleague Marisol Quevedo Rerucha, author of *Beyond the Surface of Restorative Practices: Building a Culture of Equity, Connection, and Healing*. Like the rest of the country, we had been through a lot, and we desperately needed to reset—to reconnect and affirm our core values. Each person shared two or three important collaboration values. After compiling and discussing individual values, we slowly agreed on 10 of them. We now start every collaborative session by grounding ourselves in our core beliefs. Additionally, we use these beliefs and agreements to guide collective decision-making and engage in difficult conversations.

Co-constructing core beliefs driven by each stakeholder's personal and cultural values is essential when defining your organization's greater moral purpose. Families and students must also be at the table during the process. We must relentlessly ensure that the individuals who represent our most historically misrepresented stakeholders use their voices during collective decision-making processes. Deeply ingrained core beliefs guide your organization's actions, driven by each person's lived experiences and cultural identities. Core beliefs define the greater purpose of your teams.

## Model of Success: The Core Collaborative Learning Network

### The Core Collaborative Core Beliefs

· We believe quality relationships are essential.

· We believe empathy has transformative power.

· We believe collaboration is key to growth and success.

· We believe belonging is a human right, and we are responsible for protecting and nurturing it.

· We believe each person has intrinsic value. We honor the dignity of ourselves and others.

· We believe all learners have voices that should be heard; if we listen, they will lead the way.

· We believe creativity is inherent in all of us, and our collective creativity is crucial for effective problem solving.

· We believe every human being deserves access to an equitable, personalized education, acknowledging that every learner and learning path is unique.

· We believe when one of us does better, we all do better.

· We believe connection is at our core and gives our relationships strength; it is the energy we share when we feel seen, heard, and valued.

## Personal Reflection:

☐ Why is it important to co-construct core beliefs with all stakeholders?

☐ How would you describe your school or system's formal and informal social networks?

☐ How do you ensure that all stakeholders take part in the process (families, students, educators, and staff)?

☐ How do you remain focused on your team's core beliefs?

# RELATIONAL TRUST

Relational trust is the connective tissue of working relationships. It is central to building effective learning communities (Bryk & Schneider, 2002). Do not underestimate the importance of trust in the learning process. Bryk and Schneider identified important determinants of relational trust: respect, personal regard for others, competence, and integrity. Respect relates to genuinely listening and valuing the opinions of others. Learning can be risky business, exposing our lack of knowledge and failures—and the need to learn from our mistakes. Relational trust grounds itself in social respect. Without respect, collaborative learning ceases.

## Strengthening Trust With Collective Agreements:

Co-designing collective agreements with as many of your stakeholders (parents, educators, staff) as possible is wildly important when ensuring an inclusive climate. Collective agreements guide all of your team's actions and serve as your cultural cornerstones. Marisol used a similar process with our team when developing our collective core beliefs agreements. She guided us in determining our individual beliefs, and then we co-designed collective agreements. We are far from perfect. However, our collective agreements ground us in who we strive to be. When we are not our best, we revisit them to get unstuck and inspired. Here is an example of our learning organization's collective agreements.

## Model of Success: The Core Collaborative Learning Network

### The Core Collaborative Community Agreements

· We honor, love, and accept ourselves and each other.

· We value our individual and collective experiences and cultures as assets.

· We are honest, loving, and supportive even when it's challenging.

· We accept that we can control only our actions and responses.

· We take ownership of the impact of our words and actions.

· We communicate bravely and responsibly, with dignity and reciprocity.

· We engage in dialogue, ask questions, and restate our understanding to ensure content and intent clarity.

· We practice shared decision-making that values all voices and ideas.

· We acknowledge that our authentic learning process includes feedback, patience, failure, success, and perseverance.

· We use a restorative approach to resolve conflict and repair harm.

It is essential to have families at the table and (in person or virtually) co-constructing collective agreements just like the co-design process focused on core beliefs. Rerucha (2021) explains,

> Collectively, these foundational statements set the tone for your organization's culture where the restorative heartset and mindset live. Having these collectively created statements helps during difficult and challenging times. They act like anchors to ground discussions and decisions. (p. 32)

We strengthen relational trust when we hear and value all voices in collective decision-making. Moral purpose and relational trust interconnect. As Bryk and Schneider (2022) explain, "Moral purpose ties us to impact and the courage that is required to make choices that lead to the greatest difference in improving student outcomes." The shared decision-making process should align schoolwide decisions and collective agreements.

## Personal Reflection:

☐ What is the purpose of co-constructing your community's collective agreements?

☐ Why is it important to include families and students when co-constructing these agreements?

☐ How do you ensure that your community agreements guide your actions?

**Tip 3.3: Co-Constructing Community Agreements:** Marisol Quevedo Rerucha describes a process for co-designing core beliefs and collective agreements in chapter 3 of her book, *Beyond the Surface of Restorative Practices*. Chapter 3 of her book coaches Impact Teams, schools, and district stakeholders through an inside-out process that honors each person's cultural identity. All stakeholders (families, students, and educators) co-design core beliefs and collective agreements, ensuring an inclusive climate and culture. When co-constructing beliefs and agreements with stakeholders, everyone must have the opportunity to express their agreement or disagreement. Marisol explains that this process takes time. She describes how frustrated you feel because you work against the clock. However, this work and time is well spent. People feel that you value them when you take their voices and input into consideration.

## Talking About Relational Trust:

It is essential to build trust within the school community. Trust-building takes time, but effective peer facilitation accelerates it. Peer facilitators model and use facilitation moves to ensure shared decision-making, active listening, risk-taking, open interactions, and goal consensus. Being intentional about measuring and monitoring team trust is essential for the ITM. You can use various available tools as entry points to open dialogue about the degree of relational trust in the learning network, as well as identify and repair harm. "Not talking" about strengthening relational trust is the perfect way to erode trust in your organization. All organizations have trust issues. However, learning networks prioritizing relational trust have stronger connections and quality relationships, leading to more risk-taking and innovation.

 **Tip 3.4: Talk About Team Trust:** Have your team take the team trust survey in the online appendix. Then discuss and acknowledge your greatest strengths and determine opportunities to enhance your relational trust.

## Personal Reflection:

☐ Why is relational trust important to you personally and professionally?

☐ How does your organization talk about trust?

☐ What intentional and transparent strategies have you put into place to strengthen trust?

## COMMUNICATION

Quality communication starts with active listening. In *Amplify Learner Voice through Culturally Responsive and Sustaining Assessment* (Bloomberg et al., 2023, pp. 98–99), the authors describe active listening as the practice of listening to understand what someone is saying. It falls under the category of empathetic listening. Active listening helps you build strong relationships and gain a deeper understanding of your students' and colleagues' perspectives.

When you practice active listening, you focus on what the other person says instead of planning a response, as you would in a debate. You paraphrase what you heard to the other person to confirm you understand. Depending on the conversation, you can ask a specific, open-ended question to dig deeper into the topic.

Active listening helps you have more meaningful and engaged conversations with learners. You develop more effective communication skills when you pay full attention—without planning what you want to say or interrupting them. We must genuinely get to know our students to create quality learning partnerships with them.

Building a restorative culture, anchored in the tenets of restorative practices, increases the cultural shifts necessary for vulnerable, transparent communication. Values that underpin restorative practice include empowerment, honesty, respect, engagement, voluntarism, healing, restoration, personal accountability, inclusiveness, collaboration, and problem-solving (Restorative Justice Consortium, 2004, p. 2). A proactive restorative culture allows individuals to feel heard when conflicts arise. This approach provides a safe forum for students and adults to express their feelings and needs. It builds relationships and communities.

| **Model of Success: Developing a Restorative Culture** <br> **Encore Performing Arts School, Victorville, CA** | |
| --- | --- |
|  | In Video 3.2, watch principal St. Claire Adriaan speaking about the importance of building a restorative culture. Learn how he collaborates with stakeholders to create a culture of belonging and inclusion. |

Without quality communication systems, learning networks become fragmented and diluted. A lack of quality communication (anchored in collective agreements, core beliefs, and decision-making) results in confusion, chaos, and mistrust. It also impacts the quality implementation of any schoolwide learning goal. Use the following elements to develop quality communication that improves both formal and informal learning networks.

- Co-construct collective agreements and shared beliefs that guide expectations
- Adopt a restorative approach to improve relational literacy and repair harm
- Share decision-making and follow through on decisions made by the most impacted group
- Engage in regular dialogues about trust.
- Be intentional with all stakeholders about the value of relational trust within a system. (You can use climate data as an excellent way to begin these conversations.)
- Establish agreed-upon, systemized, transparent, and supportive reciprocal communication systems

**Tip 3.5:** Improve quality communication with these ed-tech tips:
- Consider using applications like Google Chat or Slack for more transparent, efficient, and reciprocal communication. Many teams collaborate asynchronously, which works well with educators' demanding schedules.
- Help parents partner with the school by offering virtual opportunities. Parents have hectic schedules and often, they need help.
- Consider project management tools like Basecamp or Asana to support communication and team management.

Remember, developing collaborative expertise lies at the heart of the ITM. Without quality communication, sharing, and building knowledge, our collective assets will become diluted.

## NUTSHELL

Cultivating a teaming culture maximizes and realizes continuous improvement goals. A learning network grounds itself in common purposes and beliefs, collective agreements, relational trust, quality relationships and connections, and an ongoing, reciprocal communication system that supports sharing and building knowledge. Understanding impact and strategically responding is what Impact Teams do. This transparent, collaborative process deepens learning, alters perspective, and demands greater attention to more asset-based teaching and learning methods. Educators, students, and families build their knowledge by building on their assets and learning together. Taking collective action based on their learning strengthens their belief in their capacity to make a difference. This teaming builds collective efficacy.

## Team Reflection:

How would your team members respond to the following questions?

- ☐ What is your team's or community's moral purpose?
- ☐ How can you leverage your informal social networks to improve knowledge-building and sharing?
- ☐ How can you increase transparency among team members and the greater community?
- ☐ What practices can you adopt to strengthen quality communication among all stakeholders?
- ☐ How do you learn about your students' and families' assets?

## Equity Reflection:

- ☐ What voice, power, and participation patterns do we notice on our team?
- ☐ How do we make it safe to share honest truths, take risks, and seek support?
- ☐ How do our identities and experiences shape our collaboration and communication?

## CHECK-IN

Use the rubric below with your team to reflect on the current state of your school. Add ideas and next steps for enhancing collaborative practices.

| Learning Network | Not Yet | Sometimes | Often |
|---|---|---|---|
| Determine common purposes to strengthen efficacy and agency for all learners. | | | |
| Co-construct shared values and collective agreements connected to our moral purpose. | | | |
| Assess relational trust at least two times per year and determine strategies to strengthen trust. | | | |
| Adopt restorative circles to cultivate quality communication with adults and students and support conflict resolution. | | | |
| Establish transparent, consistent, and reciprocal communication systems (cloud service, Google Chat, Slack, Zoom, etc.) | | | |
| What's next? | | | |

**Models of Success: Chapter 3: Cultivating a Teaming Culture**

**Overview: The videos and resources in this chapter illustrate the transformation of a traditional professional learning community (PLC) into a student-centered model.**

**Video 3.3**
**Model of Success: Developing a Learner Profile**
**Mammoth Unified School District, Mammoth Lakes, CA**

Dr. Jennifer Wildman, former superintendent of Mammoth Unified School District in Mammoth Lakes, illustrates developing a self-empowered learner profile with her community.

# TEAMING
# TO LEARN

Every art and every inquiry, and similarly every action and choice, is thought to aim at some good; and for this reason, the good has rightly been declared to be that at which all things aim.

Aristotle

## Mastery Moment

Consider a time you felt curious about something. What led to your curiosity? How did you feel? What motivated you to learn?

# THE *WHAT:* TEAMING TO LEARN FOR COLLABORATIVE INQUIRY

If our goal is to advance student agency, we must advance educator agency. Self-empowerment resides at the center of collaborative inquiry, and *inquiry* is the heart of a robust and compassionate learning environment. Creating a learning culture that engages *all* school community members in inquiry, investigation, and innovation requires teachers to take the lead. This means that district and school leaders must formally and informally advocate for teacher voices and model key learning habits, including empathy, problem-solving, perseverance, and patience. Teacher teams focus on cultivating these academic and social-emotional mindsets through collaborative inquiry that puts "learning" at the center. In addition, educators must formally and informally advocate for student and family voices and create opportunities for collective decision-making when coming to a consensus on school and district learning goals and the strategies to realize their goals. The Impact Team Model (ITM) reimagines traditional professional learning communities (PLCs) and other school-district learning teams in two specific areas.

1. It includes a critical partnership between educators, students, and families in quality implementation of the formative assessment process anchored in their collective core beliefs.

2. Learning authentically together to scale up evidence-based practices through collaborative inquiry grounded in the tenets design thinking.

The Impact Team Model emphasizes personal and professional growth, strong and authentic connections, a sense of personal and collective efficacy, and creating meaningful work *together*.

## PUZZLES VERSUS PROBLEMS

Schools are filled with challenges and obstacles. Many educators approach these challenges as puzzles, while others view these obstacles as problems. Impact Teams use strengths-based approaches to solve learner agency 'puzzles of practice.' The biggest difference between solving a *puzzle* and solving a *problem* is how you experience the process. The process of solving a puzzle begins with a picture that you are trying to create (Scott, 2008). However, when teams are faced with problems, it is often difficult to visualize the solution. This is because you start your journey with a laser-like focus on the problem instead of launching your inquiry with an aspirational picture in mind. To ensure the vision represents a shared image of success for the entire team, it is important that a variety of voices co-construct it, including the people that have been harmed most by the system.

## CO-DESIGNING A VISION FOR SELF-EMPOWERMENT

Impact Teams envision success before they begin their inquiry. They build a shared vision of the future. They dream big and imagine how success will look, sound, and feel if they wildly succeed. Every stakeholder needs to be an artist, collaboratively painting a picture that defines the characteristics of a self-empowered learner.

## Personal Reflection:

☐  What are some self-empowerment characteristics?

You may think of someone who beat the odds. Whatever the case, you may have seen these qualities or characteristics bubble to the surface.

- perseverance
- flexible thinking
- thinking about thinking (metacognition)
- clear communication
- resilience
- determination
- openness to continuous learning
- self-trust
- vulnerability
- humility
- love
- empathy

If we have a shared vision of success grounded in community values, solving 'puzzles of practice' will be fulfilling, exhilarating, and exciting.

## DEVELOPING AN INQUIRY-DRIVEN MINDSET

In Chapter 3, we discussed co-designing core beliefs with all stakeholders. Everyone rows in the same direction, regardless of the bends in the river. Core beliefs ground successful inquiry. All members of a learning community must share an understanding of what they are aiming to learn together. They must be united in their vision and have clarity of the success criteria they must embody to reach their ambitious goals. When educators partner in collaborative inquiry, they understand quality learning, generate evidence of what works, decide on the next steps, and take collective action for continuous improvement.

Educators, students, and families are a school's greatest resource for innovation. What is needed, quite simply, is for teachers to be given the time to share best practices, experiment with high-impact strategies, investigate and innovate, and learn together. "As teachers in a school feel empowered to do great things, great things happen" (Eells, 2011).

If we want to advance student agency, teacher teams need autonomy and the decision-making power to do what is right for their students and families. When teachers develop inquiry-driven mindsets, they curiously ask questions. Genuine questions come to mind.

- What is the purpose of propelling our inquiry? How will we learn, and what 'puzzles of practice' will we solve together?
- How will inquiry allow *everyone* to follow their passions, dreams, and ambitions?
- How does inquiry enable the development of knowledge, skills, dispositions, and courage that puts students in the driver's seat?
- How can we positively impact students who have been harmed the most?
- What formative assessment practices will strengthen our team?
- How can we invent new teaching tools and improve existing ideas?
- What practices can we release to make space for learner ownership?
- How can we contribute positively to others?

The team's curiosity fuels their inquiry. Teams collect multiple sources of evidence, analyze it, and take action based on their findings. Collaborative inquiry is not linear; it is iterative. Since inquiry-based learning can feel messy, Impact Teams need trained peer facilitators to thrive. Quality peer facilitation helps teams focus discussions, propels energy forward, and fosters authentic accountability. Genuine interest fuels the findings. Impact Teams move from where they begin to where they want to be in the future through curiosity, well-designed inquiry, and a shared vision of success.

## EFFECTIVE AND FOCUSED LEARNING TEAMS

For inquiry to prosper, we need effective and focused learning teams that share knowledge, share advice, and build upon existing knowledge. We know exactly what makes teacher teams productive (and what does not). The teams with the most impact have clear goals and relentlessly pursue them. The author of *Collaborative Leadership: Six Influences That Matter Most*, Peter Dewitt, states "Leaders need to make sure that teachers are working on goals that they actually care about, and not on goals that they think the leader wants them to achieve. …teachers will find much more success if they work on the goals they are personally motivated to work on." (2017, p. 124) Autonomous Impact Teams determine their inquiry focus and build goal consensus from the very beginning. Gallimore and colleagues (2009) cite five components to support effective teaming.

1. Job-alike teams (a common relevant focus)

2. Clear goals

3. A trained peer facilitator

4. Inquiry-based protocols

5. Stable settings (a principal who commits to protected time)

Recently, a paper out of Harvard Graduate School of Education by Johnson, Reinhorn, and Simon (Shafer, 2016) examined optimal collaboration, listing the following five factors.

1. A clear, worthwhile purpose

2. Sufficient regular time

3. Administrative support and attention

4. Trained teacher facilitators

5. An integrated approach to teacher support

When you compare both studies, you notice similar elements that drive the Impact Team Model.

## EIGHT ELEMENTS THAT DRIVE IMPACT TEAMS

The Impact Team Model combines eight elements. We wove

these threads throughout the model.

1. High expectations and goal consensus that strengthen learner efficacy and agency

2. Strengthened relational trust and belonging that leverages formal and informal social networks

3. A leadership team and principal that protect, promote, and participate in team learning and development

4. Knowledge about strengths (in ourselves, students, families, educators, staff, community)

5. Teacher agency through shared decision-making

6. Invested time and resources for quality peer facilitation

7. Focus, equitable communication, and knowledge sharing and building  for all tiers of support

8. Understanding impact and taking action using purposeful, descriptive feedback grounded in asset-based practices

These elements also informed Jenni Donohoo, author of *Collective Efficacy: How Educators' Beliefs Impact Student Learning* (2017). Donohoo's six conditions reflect this section's eight ITM elements and related factors. (See Chapter 2.) Nurture and tend to these elements intentionally as your teams implement the Impact Team Model.

# THE *WHY:* RESEARCH AND REASONS

Developing collective capacity through collaborative inquiry transforms schools into learning organizations instead of teaching factories. Collaborative inquiry provides a solution-driven process to reach our collective potential and meet today's diverse needs. Although there are many reasons to team up, we have highlighted the following four reasons why collaborative inquiry is the most effective job-embedded professional learning:

## REASON 1: LEARNING TEAMS CONTRIBUTE SIGNIFICANTLY TO SCHOOL IMPROVEMENT.

In a 5-year study of Title I schools that serve more than 14,000 students, Gallimore et al. (2009) found that teacher-learning teams contributed significantly to overall school improvement. After converting routine meetings to teacher-learning teams focusing on student learning, achievement rose by 41% overall and by 54% for Hispanic students.

Schools only improve when they constantly learn. Collaborative inquiry and action research drive ongoing, job-embedded professional learning. Impact Teams strategically build collaborative expertise among all stakeholders through dynamic and deep collaborative learning.

## REASON 2: COLLABORATION DEEPENS TEACHERS' ABILITY TO ASSESS FOR UNDERSTANDING.

Grade-level teams that create student assessment portfolios deepen their knowledge about assessing student understanding. They use assessment results to guide their instruction (Gearhart and Osmundson, 2008).

## REASON 3: REFINING PEDAGOGICAL PRACTICES INCREASES STUDENT LEARNING.

When teachers collaboratively microteach, a video review of lessons, they more than double the speed of student learning (Hattie, 2023). They use the ITM Microteaching Protocol to get feedback from each other that refines and enhances practice.

## REASON 4: COLLABORATIVE INQUIRY IMPROVES DATA-DRIVEN DECISION-MAKING.

Teachers are more likely to collect and use data systematically when working as a group when using high school collaborative inquiry (Ingram and colleagues (2004). Teachers tend to rely on anecdotes and intuition when working independently. Groupthink works!

# THE *HOW:* THE IMPACT TEAM MODEL ARCHITECTURE

We presented the architecture and health of your learning network in Chapter 3. Here, we unpack Impact Team processes and structures.

· The learning network
· **The process**
· **The structure**

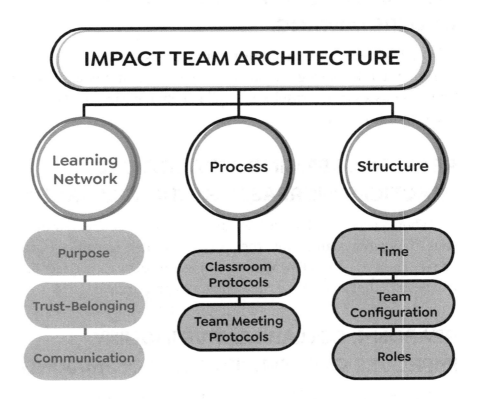

# IMPACT TEAM PROCESSES

## Activating Collaborative Inquiry Through Design Thinking

Impact Teams use a collaborative inquiry process anchored in the tenets of design thinking (or human-centered design). "Design thinking is different from other innovation and ideation processes in that it is solution-based and user-centric rather than problem-centric. This means it focuses on the solution to a problem instead of the problem itself" (Brown, 2008). Impact Teams focus on understanding the needs of students and families by generating innovative, evidence-based solutions, and testing and refining ideas. The Impact Team design thinking process (see Figure 4.1) consists of several stages, each with its own purpose. Each stage considers different tools and protocols to guarantee knowledge sharing and building. Teams grow their collaborative expertise. As teams plan for their inquiry, they use design thinking  stages to organize data, goals, and theory of action about learner agency. All teams (ILTs, PLCs, equity, SEL, and district level) can use our blueprint design. However, the 'puzzles of practice' will differ based on your team's purpose. Use the blueprint process to plan robust inquiry that supports a quality implementation of the Impact Team architecture.

**Figure 4.1: Design Thinking**

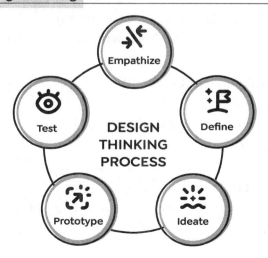

## Inquiry Blueprint Planning Stages.

**1. Empathize: Teams gather evidence from students and families using empathetic methods.**

During this stage, Impact Team designers seek to understand the needs, motivations, and challenges of students, families, and communities. Empathy is the critical starting point for successful design thinking. Teams need to know who will benefit from solving the problem. Understanding your students' and families' assets and needs is key to ensuring progress.

Teams focus their energy on improving the learning lives of absolutely every learner. Impact Teams engage in empathetic research methods such as observations, interviews, and surveys to gain insights about what it is like to be a learner and a student within the class and the greater school community. Understanding students' and families' assets, needs, barriers, attitudes, and aspirations unlocks innovation and new opportunities. Observing and engaging with students helps them understand and internalize their learning experiences emotionally and psychologically. This equips teams to design psychologically safe solutions, a key source of self-efficacy. During this stage, team members become aware of their assumptions and implicit biases to gather relevant insights about learning challenges and actionable items.

**Example: Blue Wave Middle School diligently closed multilingual learners (ML) opportunity gaps in English Language Arts (ELA). The ELA Team met with each parent one-on-one to determine student strengths. They used these questions.**

• What are your child's strengths?
• What do they love to learn about?
• How do they learn best when at home?
• What makes you most proud?
• What kind of support do you need to help your child?
• When is the best time to reach you?
• If you had one wish for your child at school, what would it be?

**The ELA team also met one-on-one with all ML students who were not making adequate growth on their ACCESS goals (Assessing Comprehension and Communication in English State-to-State for English Language Learners). They asked these questions.**

• What do you love to learn about?
• How do you learn best?
• What do you do when you are stuck?
• How do you ask for help?
• How do you use your home language to learn English?
• Describe one wish that would make learning better for you.
• What questions do you have about your ACCESS score and next steps?

**Abbreviated Parent Findings.**

• families had a lot of information about what their kids like to learn and their kids' strengths.
• Most students helped a lot around the house with younger siblings and chores.
• Many families spoke about their child's love of playing video games, using TikTok, playing sports, or playing with family and friends.
• Most students did their homework at home, but families found it very hard to support them with homework in English.
• Families were open to supporting their kids in their home language.
• Families overwhelmingly wanted to help their children attain English but also needed ESL support.
• It helped to explain the meaning behind ACCESS scores in one-on-one parent conversations.

**Abbreviated Student Findings:**

• Most students loved learning things on TikTok or YouTube.
• Most like learning from other friends. They also liked lots of examples.
• Most only had a few strategies in their toolkit if they got stuck outside of asking the teacher.
• Most wished they had more time to collaborate with friends to discuss their learning.
• Many also wished they had more choices in school and didn't like doing homework because they were unsure how to do it.
• Many reported that it was hard to ask for help.

## 2. Define: Use data triangulation to define a 'puzzle practice.'

During this stage, Impact Teams analyze the information they gathered in the first stage. They identify the puzzles they need to solve. They synthesize "empathetic data" from Stage 1 and triangulate it with performance data to make sense of the landscape.

Teams determine themes and patterns that bubble to the surface. They look for unmet student needs and define any unexpected barriers that may shift their focus. They reflect on the questions to ensure they ask the *right* questions. Teams reassess their assumptions to mitigate implicit bias. Teams develop baseline evidence statements that summarize the evidence using their data triangulation. These baseline evidence statements help them move into the ideation stage.

---

**Example: Blue Wave Middle School's seventh-grade ELA Team triangulated student and family voice data (Stage 1) with four more sources of evidence. They used the Analysis of Evidence (AOE) Protocol.**

· State assessment data
· Universal screener
· ACCESS: Summative assessments for language acquisition
· DESSA SEL Screening Tool

**Baseline Evidence Statements:**

· State test results indicated that 60% of students scored well when pulling key ideas and details from a text.
· Forty percent of students proficiently determined the meanings of unknown words and used text structure for comprehension, focusing on craft and structure.

**Our universal screener tightly aligns with state test results. (It essentially says the same thing.)**

  □ The MAP (Measures of Academic Progress) test does group the students based on needs. Most of the students needing extra support are multilingual learners.
· Thirty-eight percent of the MLs lay on the expanding ACCESS level. (They mostly needed support in the reading and writing domain.)

- DESSA illustrated the following strengths and opportunities for the ML demographic group.
  - Strengths: Personal Responsibility, Decision-Making, and Self-Management.
  - Opportunities: Optimistic Thinking, Relationship Skills, Social Awareness, and Self-Awareness
- The team reviewed student and family voice data

### 3. Ideate: Teams brainstorm evidence-based solutions.

This stage focuses on generating a wide range of creative ideas and potential solutions anchored in evidence-based practices to advance learner agency. This messy stage requires suspending judgment to foster innovation.

It is key to create an Impact Team learning space that embraces and assesses divergent and provocative solutions. They converge on a few of the strongest pathways for the team to pursue. Impact Team designers employ brainstorming techniques, sketching, prototyping, and other divergent thinking methods to encourage a free flow of ideas. Teams use tools like a SWOT analysis (strengths, weaknesses, opportunities, and threats) or a prioritization matrix to build confidence in solution pathways viability.

**Example: The Blue Wave ELA Team brainstormed these possible solutions for advancing learner agency. They based it on the 'puzzles of practice' they found during the previous stages. They brainstormed these possible solutions.**

- Annotation of Text to support craft needs (vocabulary and text structure)
  - Context Clues
  - Labeling Text Structure and Purpose
- Video lessons. Kids could also make priority standards "How To" videos
- Peer assessments since they liked to learn with friends. It also helped teachers receive more feedback

**They then aligned their ideas to the Visible Learning research to determine if they could maximize student learning. They partnered with an Impact Team coach to determine if their ideas were valid and reliable.**

- Text Annotation: Highlighting and Underlining .44 ES
- Peer Tutoring: .51
- Reciprocal Teaching: .74
- Peer and Self-Grading: .54
- Success Criteria: .64
- Feedback (Tasks and Processes): .63
- Classroom Discussion: .82

**4. Prototype: Impact Teams develop a theory of action.**

During the prototype stage, Impact Teams develop a theory of action, determine their evidence base, develop SMART goals, and envision success.

- **Theory of Action:** During the prototype stage, Impact Team designers transform and narrow their solution pathways into tangible representations. They create a theory of action. A theory of action (TOA) proposes what may happen after implementing a strategy set. Developing a TOA requires shared decision-making and critical judgment about which strategic actions will lead to a positive impact. A TOA helps team members connect what they plan with what they hope to get. They refine, improve, re-design, and revise proposed solutions through team reviews and critiques. Prototyping helps test and refine ideas, gather feedback, and make necessary iterations before proceeding to the next stage.
- **Determine Evidence Base:** Teams determine what evidence they will need to triangulate and analyze. Will their prototype and theory of action have a positive impact? The teams' choice of evidence must align with their TOA or inquiry question.
- **Develop SMART Goals:** They develop SMART goals (specific, measurable, achievable, relevant, and time-bound) to ensure inquiry moves forward. It helps with timing and accountability.
- **Envision Success:** When teams complete a prototype, they envision success. Stephen Covey (2020) bases one of his seven habits—beginning with the end in mind—on imagination: "the ability to envision in your mind what you cannot at present

see with your eyes." According to Covey, we create all things twice: a mental model (where one envisions their goal and imagines achievement), and a second (or physical creation) that follows a blueprint. If they wildly succeed, teams co-construct what students will say, think, feel, and do.

· **Determine Protocols:** Teams begin early protocol discussions to guide their inquiry. They discuss possible protocols that will maximize team learning outcomes.

---

**Example: Blue Wave Middle School ELA Team**

· **Theory of Action:** If we engage our students in learning how to annotate text coupled with peer review, then they will develop their expertise in figuring out words they don't know and use text structures to make meaning. Then they will build capacities in oral language development, self-regulation, and metacognition through peer review and accountable talk.

· **Evidence Base:** We will progress monitor our inquiry by collecting and analyzing the following evidence to gauge a positive impact.
  □ Student self- and peer assessments 3 or 4 times annually
  □ Universal screener data on priority standards
  □ Common formative assessment data aligned to priority standards
  □ DESSA data to build capacity with the competencies of self-awareness, optimistic thinking, and goal-directed behavior

· SMART Goal: 35% of our MLs at the overall expanding level will increase their language proficiency by one ACCESS level. We will increase MAP growth by 35% for this same group of students by the end of the year. We will use common formative assessments (CFAs) to monitor progress between MAP assessment windows.

· Envision Success: (abbreviated for this example)
  □ Students annotate text with validity and reliability.
  □ They will use annotations to support meaning-making.
  □ They will partner up to check annotation quality through peer review.
  □ They will use academic vocabulary when engaging in peer review.

---

## 5. Investigate: Impact Teams monitor impact and progress and then take action.

This stage aims to gather feedback (qualitative and quantitative) and insights by testing the prototype with students using the Impact Team 10 purposeful protocols (described later in this chapter). Impact Teams monitor progress through the Analysis of Evidence (AOE) Protocol and through observation of visible impact. Then, evaluate their impact and make midcourse adjustments when necessary. While monitoring progress, Impact Teams use open-ended, solution-focused questions to avoid shutting down iterative improvement.

- What works well? Evidence?
- What is going so-so? Evidence?
- What do we need to develop?
- What do the students think about the process? Do they see improvement in themselves as learners?
- What did we learn together?

Teams monitor their inquiry using quantitative methods like interim, formative, and summative assessment. They use qualitative methods such as student–family focus groups, surveys, and 1:1 interviews to gain insight into the stories behind the data.

---

**Example: Blue Wave Middle School ELA Team**

- **Protocols:** We will use the Microteaching Protocol and Peer Coaching Protocol to refine text annotation and peer review expertise. We will use the Analysis of Evidence (AOE) Protocol to monitor universal screener, annotation, and CFA progress.

---

 **Tip 4.1:** Check the online appendix for the Impact Team 'inquiry planning blueprint' implementation rubric.

## Team Reflection:

- ☐ What is similar and different in how your team plans for collaborative inquiry?
- ☐ Why is it important to use empathetic methods so early in the design thinking process?
- ☐ What resonated with you most about the inquiry blueprint planning process?

**Tip 4.2: Models of Success**: Check out inquiry models of success from schools nationwide at the end of this chapter.

# PROTOCOLS DRIVE THE INQUIRY PROCESS

As teams launch their inquiry, they determine what protocols they will use to monitor their goals. We categorized the protocols by context.

## Team Protocols:

Teams need rules of engagement and structures for focused and effective knowledge sharing and building collaborative expertise. Team meeting protocols were born out of what effective teams need.

- Get to know standards or create criterion-based formative tasks
- Calibrate student work samples for proficiency
- Share, try, and refine innovative teaching strategies
- Engaging in lesson study, video lesson reviews (micro-teaching), and peer coaching
- Apply the formative assessment process in partnership with students
- Analyze the work analysis and other key evidence sources
- Determine collective research-based actions

## Classroom Protocols:

Routines and processes are the backbone of daily classroom life. Quality routines make it easier for students and teachers to learn and achieve. Classroom protocols guide students in these areas.

- Understanding learning intentions
- Co-constructing success criteria
- Giving and receiving evidence-based feedback
- Articulating learning processes (surface, deep, and transfer levels)

· Engaging in effective self- and peer-assessment using accountable talk
· Activating reflection and goal-setting

# 10 PURPOSEFUL PROTOCOLS AND THE EAA FRAMEWORK

We designed and adapted the ITM's 10 purposeful protocols
from common protocols we used as educators and school leaders.
Our teams field tested the protocols nationally, ensuring efficiency
and practicality (since teachers have limited time). We infused
video observations into many of our protocols as an efficient, powerful medium to enhance teaching and learning. We anchored all
ITM protocols in the Evidence–Analysis–Action (EAA) process. (See
Chapter 1.) Teams use quality Evidence to Analyze the impact on
learners. EAA sets the team up for inquiry and action research.
Quite simply, EAA is how we do business. (See Figure 4.2).

**Figure 4.2: EAA and the Impact Team Purposeful Protocols**

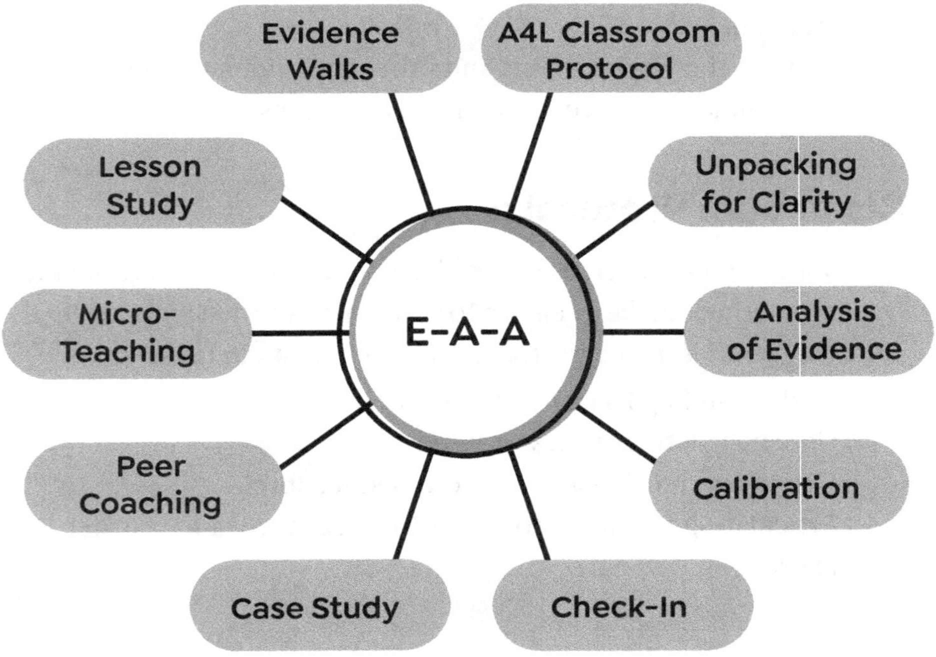

The EAA protocols serve four purposes. They (1) triangulate and analyze data, (2) refine and enhance pedagogy, (3) advance equity and inclusion, and (4) ensure quality implementation of core formative practices. Each protocol purposefully serves as a vehicle for building collaborative expertise that advances learner ownership and agency.

## Figure 4.3: Purposes for Protocols

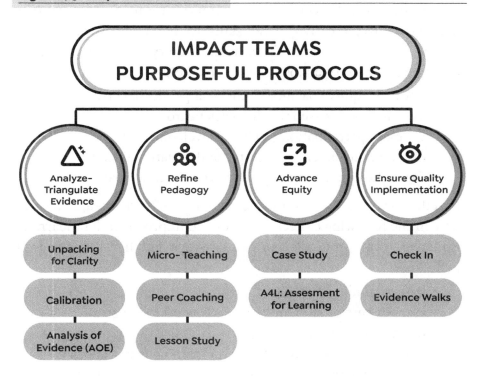

Since the ITM is driven to refine, enhance, and ensure quality implementation of the core formative practices (learning intentions, success criteria, questioning, accountable talk, feedback, self-and peer assessment, reflection, and goal setting), many protocols are used in the classroom setting to promote and refine metacognition and self-regulation. Microteaching, Peer Coaching, and Lesson Study Protocols are used within the classroom and are anchored in the A4L Classroom Protocol, which will be described in detail in the online appendix.

**Tip 4.3**: Impact Teams rely on effective peer facilitation. The book *Leading Powerful Professional Learning: Responding to Complexity with Adaptive Expertise* by Le Fevre, Timperly, Tyford, and Ell provides easy-to-use, one-page deliberate acts of facilitation summaries.

## Protocols Strengthen Collaborative Expertise

Protocols create recurring opportunities for teachers to contribute knowledge, creativity, and skills to build expertise. We use protocols purposefully to focus team inquiry and stimulate deep thinking and quality dialogue. Protocols help:

- advance equity (balance traditional power structures)
- establish transparency (all voices heard)
- promote participation (all voices welcome)
- distribute leadership (multiple and situational leaders)
- focus the conversation (stick to the learning goal)

Based on the research and our experience, effective teams participate in the following collective actions to improve student learning. Effective team protocols consist of steps familiar to educators, including:

- joint goal identification
- assessments of student progress toward those goals
- research-based approaches
- multiple-source feedback to plan learning experiences
- team biases and assumptions when analyzing student work
- differentiating and personalizing instruction for all MTSS tiers of support
- strengthening relational literacy and belonging

**Tip 4.4**: In Video 4.1, Dr. Brian Waterman, principal of Lyons Township High School, and Karen Raino, division chair, discuss the power of purposeful protocols that emphasize student learning during Impact Team meetings.

## Advancing Equity:

An overarching purpose of the ITM is to be aware of and to disrupt long-standing opportunity gaps related to assessment and grading for historically misrepresented students and families that have been harmed by the system. Although all ITM protocols advance equity and inclusion, the two protocols below engage educators and teams to solve practice puzzles within their control. These protocols refocus the path to equity, ensuring that inquiry cycles are more than just a set of meetings. They result in a visible impact on the students who need the most support.

- **A4L Classroom:** This protocol operationalizes the formative assessment process using the principles of assessment for learning (A4L) during classroom instruction. This protocol advances equity by involving students in every aspect of the assessment experience. When students engage in "assessment for learning" (A4L), they learn more about themselves and each other. They engage in reflective dialogue about where they are in their learning, their ultimate goals, and how they plan to reach their goals. When teachers and students use the three-step EAA process, they co-construct and apply learning intentions and success criteria, peer- and self-assessment, accountable talk feedback, and determining next steps. Hattie (2023) refers to this process as developing assessment-capable learners. This process nearly triples the learning rate (1.02 effect size). The A4L Classroom Protocol is unique to the ITM. We have found no other PLC frameworks that put students at the center by intentionally advancing core formative practices that are fundamental to the quality implementation of assessment for learning.

- **Case Study:** Teams use this protocol to study students who need extra support. They often need extra support due to long-standing opportunity gaps outside their control. The goal of the Case Study Protocol is two-fold: (1) discovering already possessed funds of knowledge to build personalized learning plans, and (2) removing systemic barriers within the control of the school so students can reach their full potential. Teams typically gather evidence from families about their child's learning passions and get advice from families on how their child learns best. Teams analyze all evidence and create evidence-based actions to support these students. Often, these students receive Tier 2 or Tier 3 support. Sometimes, the obstacles are systemic and require schools to revise policies to avoid harming students.

## Data Use:

These three protocols use data-driven, shared decision-making.

- **Analysis of Evidence (AOE):** Impact Teams use this three-step protocol to analyze and triangulate multiple sources of evidence. This can include student work, perception data, climate data, SEL data, universal screeners, and more. This focuses on understanding learning impacts, determining the root cause, and taking collective actions anchored in evidence-based practices. Teams collaboratively share expertise, which strengthens collective teacher efficacy. Teams can use our AOE Protocol successfully in about 45 to 50 minutes. Teams walk away with detailed, clear, and practical plans grounded in strategies with the highest effect (regarding advancing student learning and differentiating by readiness). We describe an example in Chapters 6 and 7. Teams grapple with these common questions when analyzing evidence:

  » What are these students' strengths? What led to these strengths?
  » What are our greatest opportunities to make positive impacts? Why? What can we control?
  » What assumptions do we make about students when we look at their work or data?
  » What patterns do we see when educators engage with different students?
  » Did our plan address the needs of each student?

» Who did we reach? Who didn't we reach? Why? What will we do next?

» What did we learn about ourselves, each other, and our students?

- **Unpacking for Clarity:** The team must be on the same page regarding learning outcomes to align their approaches to meeting standards. This protocol ensures teams understand how to partner with students in the formative assessment process. It engages teams in

  » researching standards
  » defining the key concepts and skills for each level of rigor (surface, deep, and transfer)
  » defining cognitive rigor for formative task design
  » agreeing on relevance, big ideas, and essential understandings
  » determining key competencies
  » developing criterion-based formative assessment tasks

  This protocol differs from other unpacking or unwrapping protocols. It emphasizes learning progressions, relevant products and performances, and learning intentions and success for each level of rigor (surface, deep, and transfer levels). See Chapter 6 for an example of developing an equitable, viable, and coherent curriculum.

- **Calibration:** This protocol ensures accurately and consistently scoring student work; this is called inter-rater reliability. The formative assessment process evaluates student work based on the success criteria developed in the Unpacking for Clarity Protocol. Using student work samples from different levels, teachers anchor their understanding of progress by establishing inter-rater reliability through calibration. Find a description and example of this protocol in Chapter 7.

## Quality Implementation:

These three protocols ensure quality core formative practices (co-constructing learning intentions and success criteria, accountable talk, questioning, self-and peer assessment, reflection, revision, and goal setting).

- **Check-In:** Monitoring instructional effectiveness based on student progress is often a well-intentioned agreement forgotten during a busy school day. This protocol ensures monitoring the implementation and effectiveness of collective actions. During the cycle, teams frequently 'check in' and share successes and challenges. They make necessary course corrections.

- **Evidence Walks:** Evidence walks (much like medical rounds) help teachers and leaders look closely at specific and predetermined practices through real-time evidence, feedback, and support. Teachers and leaders observe a colleague's classroom as volunteers, looking for practice-related evidence. The team later provides nonjudgmental descriptive feedback (analysis) based on predetermined specific criteria. The team identifies the next action steps based on the feedback. Find a full protocol description in Chapter 7.

## Refining Pedagogy:

We adapted these three protocols for the ITM to enhance formative assessment. They stem from the three-step Evidence–Analysis–Action (EAA) process.

- **Microteaching:** Impact Team members try out small parts of lessons and strategies specific to the formative assessment with one another, without students present, via video. This reduces the variable of students, allowing for the practice of new strategies before trying them in the classroom. The team can view open-source videos from The Teaching Channel, Teachertube, or The Core Collaborative YouTube Channel.

The team provides positive, specific feedback. Each team member tries the observed technique. You can do this in small teams, or teachers can practice the strategy in front of everyone. Summarize learning at the end.

· **Lesson Study:** Like Microteaching, the Lesson Study Protocol improves instructional effectiveness specific to formative assessment. Teachers collaboratively examine their practice from planning to teaching, observing, and critiquing. The team creates a detailed lesson plan that one teacher teaches, and the others observe. The observation focuses on students' responses, not the teacher's actions. Afterward, the team revises the lesson.

· **Peer Coaching:** Teachers partner with an instructional coach or a peer coach to refine core formative practices. We have found that it is easier to get teacher coverage for one teacher than substitute teachers for a whole team. Peer coaching provides a practical way for teachers to refine practice in a safe, supportive environment.

 **Tip 4.5**: Find templates for each protocol in the online appendix. You can access the Impact Team website for templates and tools to assist your team with planning and conducting a collaborative inquiry.

 ## Team Reflection:

☐  What protocols does your team currently use? How do they support team learning?

# THE IMPACT TEAM STRUCTURE

The nuts and bolts of collaboration operationalize the model. Collaboration will be haphazard and hit or miss without organization. Unstructured meetings rarely result in authentic and actionable collaboration.

## Time

Impact Teams need sufficient and protected time to become effective. If time is not protected and interruptions are allowed, the ITM will not engage in learning. Interruptions convey that inquiry is not valued.

- Impact Teams meet weekly (45–60 minutes). This is *protected* time. Never supersede it with other activities. Principals in high-performing schools dedicate and protect teacher collaboration time.
- Instructional leadership teams meet monthly (60–90 minutes) to guide, support, and monitor schoolwide Impact Teams.

## Team Configuration

Configure teams based on their purpose in achieving common goals. Here are some examples.

- Elementary: grade-level teams
- Secondary: course-alike teams
- Curricular: vertical teams
- Response to Intervention (RTI) and child study to represent support services
- Instructional leadership: lead teachers and peer facilitators from all Impact Teams
- Equity teams
- SEL teams
- District teams
- Curricular teams
- Climate teams

Regardless of the team's makeup, each brings people together to generate ideas, solve problems, and learn from one another—firmly anchored in a common purpose: developing self-empowered learners.

## Roles

Teams identify and follow roles. The team determines necessary roles and creates a job description for each. We define *roles* as useful behaviors that contribute to the team's effectiveness. Each member of the team adopts a role. Create clear, defined roles and define the skills needed to function in that role. Agree on and accept the roles as a team.

We recommend the following:

- Trained peer facilitator
- Recorder
- Monitor (time and focus)
- Critical friend

 **Tip 4.6**: Check out these facilitation tips from the National Equity Project.

## NUTSHELL

Understanding impact and strategically responding is what Impact Teams do. Highly effective teacher teams include:

- shared purpose and core beliefs and collective agreements grounded in relational trust and belonging
- continuous improvement of reciprocal communication structures and processes
- design thinking that provides a human-centered process for solving practice puzzles
- purposeful protocols that ensure meetings focus on team-driven goals
- structures that guarantee teams have the time, tools, and autonomy to build collaborative expertise

This transparent, collaborative process deepens learning, alters perspective, and demands greater attention. It zeroes in on asset-based teaching and learning. Teachers build their knowledge together, and collective action strengthens their belief in their capacity to make a difference. This builds collective teacher efficacy.

## Team Reflection:

☐ How have you co-constructed your values with all stakeholders?

☐ What is the quality of your community agreements? Do you need to revisit them with everyone?

☐ What is the trust level in your school's community? How do you know? How do you strengthen relational trust?

☐ Do teams have time to engage in collaborative inquiry?

☐ What are your competing priorities? Do they have the impact you want? Do they take away from collaborative inquiry?

☐ How do your school processes ensure productivity grounded in evidence, analysis, and collective action (EAA)?

☐ What are your next steps?

## Equity Reflection:

☐ How can we leverage our intentional protocols while staying rooted in a collective purpose and relationships?

☐ How do our values and agreements help us discuss inequity concerning race, gender, and power? How do identities shape our work and collaboration?

☐ What processes or agreements can we build to address any tension or discord?

## CHECK-IN

Use the rubric below to reflect on the current state of your teams. Add ideas and next steps to enhance collaborative practices.

| Process | Not Yet | Sometimes | Always |
|---|---|---|---|
| Impact Teams plan for inquiry using the design thinking tenets. | | | |
| We use protocols based on purpose and evidence to help monitor a greater inquiry. | | | |
| Trained peer facilitators lead team meetings using purposeful, agreed-upon protocols. | | | |
| Classroom protocols anchor and enhance the formative assessment process implementation. | | | |
| Our team receives feedback on our collaborative practices and Impact Team inquiry cycle. | | | |
| What's next? | | | |
| **Structure** | **Not Yet** | **Sometimes** | **Always** |
| Impact Teams meet weekly for 45–60 minutes or more. | | | |
| Teams support common learning goals. | | | |
| We have defined roles (facilitator, recorder, monitor, critical friend, etc.). | | | |
| Peer facilitators meet consistently to improve their skills. | | | |
| What's next? | | | |

# MASTERY MOMENTS AND MODELS OF SUCCESS

**Models of Success: Impact Team Inquiry**

**Chapter 4: Teaming to Learn**

**Overview: The videos and resources in this chapter illustrate a transformation from a traditional professional learning community (PLC) structure to a student-centered model.**

| | |
|---|---|
|  | **Principal Inquiry in Staten Island School District, NYC DOE**<br><br>Dr. Marion Wilson engages her leaders in principal inquiry, ensuring professional learning engagement geared toward learner-centered systems. |
|  | **Metacognition Inquiry at Naples Street Elementary, NYC DOE**<br><br>Read how Samanta Sahota and her co-teacher Hunter Wellford focused their inquiry on closing the metacognitive equity gap with second graders. The goal: ending the stigma of "smart students" vs. "kids that need help." |
|  | **Problem-Solving Inquiry at Oakland Elementary, Spartanburg, SC**<br><br>This 2nd-grade team tackled collaborative inquiry problem-solving using microteaching and peer coaching protocols. They co-constructed criteria with students, deepened mathematics learning, and strengthened collective efficacy. |
|  | **Peer Feedback Inquiry in High School Scuba Class at Lyons Township High School District in Le Grange, IL**<br><br>Katie Smith shares the power of peer feedback in strengthening learner and collective teacher efficacy. |

**Reciprocal Teaching Inquiry at PS 9: Naples Street Elementary in the NYC DOE**

5th-grade teacher Graziella Casale uses inquiry with her 5th-grade Impact Team to close the metacognitive equity gap through reciprocal teaching.

**Self-Peer Assessment Inquiry in PS 22 in Staten Island, New York City DOE**

Learn how teacher leader Danielle DiCapua led her team into advances in self-peer assessment inquiry.

# STRENGTHENING STUDENT EFFICACY

## THE FORMATIVE ASSESSMENT PROCESS IN ACTION

**Assessment for learning happens in the classroom and involves students in every aspect of their own assessment to build their confidence and to maximize their achievement.**

Stiggins & Chappuis, 2006, p. 11

**Mastery Moment:**

Describe the best experience you have had in helping students set goals and achieve them. What conditions were in place that led to your success?

# THE *WHAT:* THE FORMATIVE ASSESSMENT PROCESS

As a young saxophonist (Paul), I worshiped Charlie Parker. I listened to records and cassette tapes (this is aging me) because I wanted to play just like Charlie. I listened and took notes on the cool licks he played. When I think about my process, I figured out success criteria based on what I valued. I used an exemplar to determine success criteria. Then, I engaged in deliberate practice using a clear mental model; I was crystal clear about my expectations. I practiced, reflected, and tried again until I could play the jazz lick proficiently. At times other saxophonists would give me feedback (peer assessment). Once a week, I went to my saxophone professor for even more feedback. We would talk about where I was stuck, he would model some key techniques, and I would try again.

Let's summarize. I understood my goal, I followed a guiding example, and I received lots of feedback. I remained focused as I practiced and reflected on my progress. The facts are clear. We professionally and personally use formative assessment. It is how we learn.

## Personal Reflection:

Think about a time in your life when you studied a model of success so you could learn something. What skills did you employ? What did you do to become successful? How is your experience similar to or different from to mine (Paul)?

# STUDENT INVOLVEMENT

Quality formative assessment involving students in every aspect of their assessment utilizes asset-based pedagogies. It effectively strengthens student efficacy. The benefits are well-documented (Margolis & McCabe, 2006). Students with strong efficacy are more likely to challenge themselves with difficult tasks and feel intrinsic motivation. They put forth a higher degree of effort to meet goals. They typically attribute failure to factors within their control rather than blaming others. Self-efficacious students recover quickly from mistakes and are more likely to achieve their goals. The Impact Team Model (ITM) utilizes quality formative assessment to create learning-focused relationships with students to assist them throughout the process.

*Formative assessment is a process, not a product!* It is not a single event or even a strategy. Assessment for learning happens in the classroom and involves students *in every assessment aspect* to build confidence and their achievement Stiggins (2007). Partnering with students in the assessment process differentiates formative assessment from most other assessments. Black and Wiliam (1998) described formative assessment as

> *activities undertaken by teachers, and by their students in assessing themselves, which provide information to be used as feedback to modify the teaching and learning activities in which they are engaged. Such assessment becomes "formative assessment" when the evidence is actually used to adapt the teaching work to meet the needs. (p. 2)*

Nationally, formative assessment has been misunderstood. It is considered a post-teaching "add-on.". However, formative assessment *is* learning and effective teaching. Quality formative assessment provides instructional frameworks for giving and receiving evidence-based feedback. Typically, many students have never been involved in the formative assessment process, but they have been tested often. Involving students in every aspect of the formative assessment process allows them to:

- compare their work to models of success
- accurately self- and peer assess
- use feedback to monitor and accelerate learning
- communicate accountably with teachers
- set and monitor realistic, accurate learning goals
- learn from mistakes
- contribute positively through reciprocal teaching and peer tutoring

**Tip 5.1: Model of Success:** It can be hard to visualize formative assessment. In video 5.1, first graders from P.S. 9 in Staten Island bring peer assessment to life. They used a Peer Assessment Rubric for bowling developed by their P.E. Teacher, Jason Ericson. Listen to principal Deanna Marco interviewing students about their learning.

## FIVE CORE PRACTICES AND MORE

International researchers identify five core quality formative assessment practices (Heritage, 2008):

1. A crucial partnership-based classroom culture with a high degree of relational trust.

2. Identified and co-constructed learning goals, intentions, and criteria, including student feedback.

3. Clearly articulated learning progressions, including subgoals.

4. Evidence-based feedback linked to success criteria.

5. Self- and peer assessment processes as multiple sources of feedback.

Although the five practices have been highlighted in the research, it is important to note that multiple Visible Learning (VL) influences are being leveraged at the same time since the VL influences are interdependent. For example, accountable talk, evaluation, and reflection are activated when students are gaining clarity of learning intentions and success criteria and/or engaging in self- and peer assessment. Figure 5.1 illustrates this concept.

**Figure 5.1 The Formative Assessment Process**

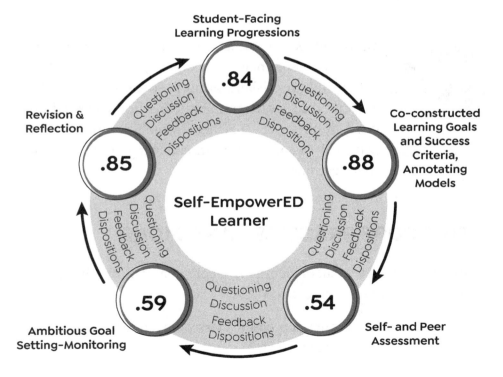

Source: *Amplify Learner Voice through Culturally Responive and Sustaining Assessment,* 2022

 **Tip 5.2**: John Almarode and Kara Vandas wrote a fantastic book called *Clarity for Learning: Five Essential Practices That Empower Students and Teachers*. There are many examples showing how teachers use the formative assessment process in partnership with students.

## CORE PRACTICE 1: LEARNING-FOCUSED RELATIONSHIPS

The student–teacher partnership is key to formative assessment. It falls flat when you do not balance power structures! Teachers and students must develop learning-focused relationships rooted in relational trust. Formative assessment puts students at the center. It promotes and prioritizes students.

## CORE PRACTICE 2: LEARNING INTENTIONS AND SUCCESS CRITERIA

Define the overarching learning goals or *intention* for the learning cycle represented in school priority standards. This may come from a state standard and other 21st-century skills (collaboration, communication, critical thinking, etc.). It may address social and emotional learning competencies, like social awareness and self-awareness. Learning intentions appear in student-friendly language. One can communicate intentions as questions or statements.

Teachers develop overarching learning intentions that focus their learning cycles. Then, they develop daily objectives aligned with the overarching learning intentions that are driven by what students need as they engage in deliberate practice. Deliberate practice engages students in intentional exercises or activities designed to build expertise in the targeted skills and knowledge needed. Deliberate practice incorporates reflection and mental models of success. Small group instruction is typically necessary because different students need different things. Learning intentions are anchored in the progression of learning (content) and strategies (process) that teachers explain and model mastery. Learning intentions are responsive to student needs and are communicated in student-friendly language. Practice makes permanence!

Success criteria ("look-fors") describe the successful attainment of a learning intention. (What does it look like during learning, and how does it look after learning it?) Quality success criteria clarifies goals for students and teachers alike. Students engage in co-constructing success criteria with student work samples. Students analyze exemplars and a range of student work. Success criteria are only as powerful as the samples. Ultimately, they identify significant performance aspects related to curriculum expectations. They can co-construct success criteria for any product, performance, process, or behavior. They can discuss it, write about it, or create diagrams driven by the standard. This allows for choice when showcasing learning.

 **Tip 5.3**: Success criteria changes the learner's experience. Listen to how enthusiastically this third-grade student speaks about his clarity and confidence since he began using co-constructed success criteria. (Video 5.2)

**Example:**
- Overarching learning intention:
- How can we clearly and concisely summarize our learning?

**Success criteria:**
- Create a clear topic sentence.
- Provide 3 or 4 key details.
  - Each detail comes from a separate.
- Use expert words.
- Paraphrase.
- Wrap up your summary that connects to the main idea.

Communicate the success criteria to students after collaborating with your teaching team. Collaboratively examine student work, analyze exemplars, and create examples *with* students using effective strategies. Begin co-constructing task success criteria aligned with the unit. This takes up substantial classroom time, but you will see tremendous benefits. You will regain the time spent on the front end, thanks to clear expectations. You will spend less time reteaching and revising. Shepard (2006) explains:

> When teachers help students to understand and internalize the standards of excellence in a discipline—that is, what makes a good history paper or a good mathematical explanation—they are helping them develop metacognitive awareness about what they need to attend to as they are writing or problem-solving. Indeed, learning the rules and forms of a discipline is part of learning the discipline, not just a means to systematize or justify grading. (p. 631)

## CORE PRACTICE 3: LEARNING PROGRESSIONS

Teachers and students determine focuses or overarching learning with intentional progressions. Learning progressions clarify the pathway used to progress in a domain. It identifies the knowledge and skills needed to reach overarching goals. The progression defines the prerequisite knowledge, skills, and pathways for the future.

Teachers co-construct and scaffold the learning progression, creating daily learning intentions or objectives aligned with the overarching learning goals of the unit of study. In addition, teachers teach students strategies or approaches to access and master the standards or competencies. A deep understanding of the learning progression allows teachers to scaffold the learning in partnership with students. The progression gives teachers and students a visible, clear pathway that ultimately supports them in making decisions about students' next learning steps.

**Tip 5.4: Model of Success:** In video 5.3, 5th grade students are engaging in quality peer assessment using a summary learning progression. Their ICT (Integrated Collaborative Teaching) teachers, Lana Regenbogen and Gabriella Pasquale recorded the video in the hallway during class at P.S. 5 in Staten Island, NY.

Individual student's progress rates may vary. Still, progressions should connect developed knowledge, concepts, and skills as they evolve from novice to experts (Heritage, 2008). This gives teachers and students explicit learning pathways. Feedback provides teachers and students with descriptive and constructive information on student progress towards their goal. Teachers and students must understand the scaffolding they will climb (Stiggins, 2005, p. 327). It also helps with identifying misconceptions and shifting mid-course to avoid derailments.

Setting overarching and daily learning intentions or goals are the critical first steps in the implementation of the formative assessment process. These learning intentions are anchored in the learning progression. Research around goal orientation indicates that students are more likely to be "challenge seekers" than "challenge avoiders" (Meyer et al., 1997). State and national standards' and SEL competencies detail what students should understand and accomplish by the end of each grade.

Communicate standards in grade-appropriate, student-friendly language. Break them down into smaller increments, particularly when differentiating for diverse needs and readiness levels. See the nonfiction writing progression in Figure 5.2 below. Note the success criteria and the example that provides clarity to students.

## Figure 5.2 Nonfiction Writing Progression

| ☆ | ☆☆ | ☆☆☆ |
|---|---|---|
| I can support the main idea:<br>• multiple facts | I can support the main idea:<br>• multiple facts<br>• definitions | I can support the main idea:<br>• multiple facts<br>• definitions<br>• text features |
| *Salt Lake City is the capital of Utah.* **The governor works in the state capitol. Utah lawmakers work in the state capitol.** | *Salt Lake City is the capital of Utah.* **The capitol building is the house of government for the U.S. state of Utah.** *The governor works in the state capitol. Also, Utah lawmakers work in the state capitol.* | *Salt Lake City is the* **capital** *of Utah. The* **capitol** *building is the house of government for the U.S. state of Utah. The governor works in the state* **capitol.** *Also, Utah lawmakers work in the state* **capitol.** |

Progressions support learner clarity for any vital skill. See the SEL progression in Figure 5.3. This progression supports learners in describing how they feel. Note the success criteria and the example below that provides clarity for learners. See other examples on our online appendix.

## Figure 5.3 SEL Progression

| ☆ | ☆☆ | ☆☆☆ | ☆☆☆☆ |
|---|---|---|---|
| I can point to an emoji to describe how I am feeling. | I can describe how I am feeling in a sentence. | I can describe how I am feeling and explain why. | I can describe how I am feeling and explain why. I can describe how to cope with my feelings. |
| | *I feel disappointed.* | *I feel disappointed that I didn't get 'first place' at 'solo and ensemble' competition.* | *I feel disappointed that I didn't get 'first place' at 'solo and ensemble' competition. I know I tried my best and I need to use the feedback from the judge to improve.* |

## Personal Reflection:

What do you learn from this example? What progressions live in your curriculum?

# CORE PRACTICE 4: EVIDENCE-BASED FEEDBACK

The formative assessment process amplifies evidence-based feedback. Deeply integrate feedback into all components of the formative assessment process. Feedback is reciprocal and derived from four sources: (1) teacher to student, (2) student to teacher, (3) peers, and (4) self.

So, what does *quality feedback* look like? Sound like? Feel like? First, we need to define "feedback." Effective feedback is rooted in the success criteria and student work. It provides critical information about where the student is, the learning goal, and what they need to do next. The litmus test: Students can answer these three questions outlined by Hattie & Timperly (2007).

1. Where am I going? (Feed-up)

2. Where am I now? (Feedback)

3. What do I need to learn next? (Feed-forward)

Since Black and Wiliam (1998) published their seminal research, *Inside the Black Box*, identifying feedback as a practice to double the rate of student learning, feedback has been recognized as being integral to student success. Effective feedback is directly connected to what criteria or competencies the student needs to know and do in relationship to mastering school and district priority standards. Nicol and Macfarlane-Dick (2005) list seven feedback principles.

1. Defines a "quality performance" (goals, criteria, and standards).

2. It facilitates the development of self-assessment.

3. It provides high-quality information to students about their learning.

4. It encourages teacher and peer dialogue focused on learning.

5. It encourages positive motivational beliefs and self-esteem.

6. It provides opportunities to close the gap between current and desired performance.

7. It provides information to teachers that can be used to help shape teaching. (p. 1)

Safety in a trusting classroom culture allows feedback to thrive. Reciprocal feedback is the *heart and soul* of the formative assessment process. It "lives" in all the Impact Team Model Purposeful Protocols.

## CORE PRACTICE 5: SELF-ASSESSMENT, PEER ASSESSMENT, AND GOAL SETTING

Students must be taught how to self- and peer assess, reflect, revise, set goals and monitor goals. "When students have consistent opportunities to develop their ability to self- and peer assess and reflect, they learn more about themselves as learners and each other." (Bloomberg et al., 2023, p. 186) Therefore, teachers must explain and model core formative assessment practices using the think-aloud strategy. Rolheiser and Ross (2000) describe a four-stage model.

- Stage 1: Define and co-construct success criteria.
- Stage 2: Teach students how to apply the criteria by explaining and modeling with samples of student work. work.
- Stage 3: Engage students in self- and peer assessment practice. Offer descriptive feedback on the quality of the process when conferencing with students.
- Stage 4: Partner with students to develop individual learning goals and action plans.

Frequently conference with students to ensure that self- and peer assessment is accurate and reliable. Giving 'feedback on feedback' ensures reliability, and it is crucial for establishing quality self- and peer assessment. It takes time, but it is well-spent time.

 **Tip 5.5: Model of Success**: Observe these fifth-grade learners from P.S. 20, the Christy J. Cugini Port Richmond School, in District 31, Staten Island, New York, as they reflect on partnerships with supportive educators. (Video 5.4)

Students set goals after receiving feedback; they take the following actions to ensure they received the feedback accurately.

- Establish individual learning goals and action plans
- Create progress and mastery e-portfolios with evidence of student learning
- Revise their work using evidence-based feedback
- Determine their strengths and next steps

Teachers must explicitly model taking action and revising based on feedback. They must model setting learning goals and giving evidence-based feedback. This establishes reliability and validity. Teachers need to hold students accountable and guide them in self-monitoring. They must also model mid-course corrections.

**Long-Term Goals:** Many schools set long-term goals based on Universal Screening data and other sources (diagnostic assessment, unit-based assessment, observations, etc.) Students typically check in weekly with an accountability partner or group. Explicitly teach students how to do this. Typically, universal screener platforms like i-Ready and NWEA MAP group students according to need. This grouping supports teachers in making goal-setting and monitoring sustainable. After modeling key processes, gradually release the responsibility to students. This does not mean that students are independent. They will need ongoing coaching until they develop expertise in the goal-setting and monitoring process.

**Short-Term Goals:** Short-term goals support progress monitoring between universal screening. Students use the success criteria from the assignment or assessment task to set individual, short-term goals. Teachers can also engage students in creating short-term unit goals anchored in each unit's learning targets. Many teachers support short term goal setting with small groups of students for efficiency. This ensures a quality collaborative experience. However, don't underestimate the power of a 1-1 conference; students need personal attention too. Consistent goal-setting rituals help students learn to monitor themselves. Many schools use their advisory periods to teach students the key tenets of goal-setting.

**Tip 5.6**: To learn more about cultural and asset-based formative assessment, read Chapter 5 of *Amplify Learner Voice through Culturally Responsive and Sustaining Assessment* by our Core Collaborative team.

# THE *WHY:* RESEARCH AND REASONS

Quality formative assessment involves students in every aspect of their own assessment and uses asset-based pedagogies that have the potential to strengthen student self-efficacy. Reflect on these five reasons.

## REASON 1: THIS PRACTICE INCREASES CONFIDENCE AND SELF-EFFICACY.

Confidence and efficacy play a role in meaningful self-assessment and goal setting. When teachers explicitly teach students how to set appropriate goals and assess their work accurately, they promote an upward learning and self-confidence cycle (Ross 2006). Demonstrating mastery strengthens self-efficacy.

## REASON 2: THIS PRACTICE INCREASES ACHIEVEMENT.

Formative assessment meta-analysis indicates significant learning gains across all content areas, knowledge and skill types, and education levels. Effect sizes for summative assessments remain consistently lower than for formative assessments (Crooks 1988). This fact emphasizes the important relationship between formative and summative assessment through the principles of backward design. Formative assessment creates conditions for clarity, evidence-based feedback and classroom discussion to flourish; these practices have the potential to accelerate learning, but most importantly they humanize the learning process.

Self-reported grading, a practice by which students assess the quality of their work or their level of mastery over a given domain, reported a 1.02 effect on learning (Hattie 2023). This effect translates into over 2 years of learning in 1 year. This involves students having clarity of the expectations so they can take ownership of their learning through setting and monitoring their goals. Each time a student reaches an ambitious goal, they have a mastery experience; this interactive process strengthens their efficacy.

## REASON 3: FORMATIVE ASSESSMENT PERSONALIZES TEACHING AND LEARNING.

The formative assessment process allows the student–teacher partnership to realize already-determined standards and competencies. Teachers and students collectively decide on the next instructional steps. Teachers can create appropriate lessons and activities for groups and individuals, and then reassess.

## REASON 4: COLLABORATIVE LEARNING INCREASES EFFICACY.

Regularly engaging in peer assessment helps students to understand their strengths and challenges. It creates ownership. Owning learning is key to engagement and motivation. Cooperative strategies have the dual outcome of improving self-efficacy *and* academic achievement (Bandura 1994).

## REASON 5: STUDENTS LEARN LIFELONG SKILLS.

The formative assessment process develops valuable lifelong skills, such as self-evaluation and self-regulation. Specifically, *self-regulation* is the capacity to alter behaviors. It enables people to adjust their actions to various social, situational, and academic demands (Baumeister & Vohs, 2007). Students learn what it takes to learn—determination, effort, and learning from mistakes.

# THE *HOW:* FOUR PURPOSEFUL PROTOCOLS TO STRENGTHEN ASSESSMENT FOR LEARNING

The ITM relies on four of the 10 EAA protocols that ensure formative assessment fidelity.

- The *A4L Classroom Protocol* communicates quality "assessment for learning" practices. Many teacher evaluation and supervision tools used nationwide align with these practices. The A4L Classroom Protocol is the heart of the ITM. Also, most state's professional learning standards for teachers anchor quality feedback and assessment practices in 'assessment for learning' practices.
  - » Danielson 3-D: Using Assessment in Instruction
  - » T-TESS: Dimension 1.4
  - » CA teacher standard 5
  - » Other district evaluation tools

- The other three protocols refine and enhance pedagogy through implementing quality assessment, as noted in the above A4L Classroom Protocol.
  - » Microteaching
  - » Lesson Study
  - » Peer Coaching

We define *fidelity* as ensuring that students are involved in every aspect. It does not imply that the implementation is linear or that every teacher has to implement it in the same way. Since classroom management is key to successful implementations, each class evolves differently. However, the five key formative assessment components provide a foundation.

# THE A4L CLASSROOM PROTOCOL UNPACKED

The ITM uses the A4L Classroom Protocol, anchored in the EAA (Evidence–Analysis–Action) framework. The protocol operationalizes the core formative assessment practices, enabling quality implementation. It has three phases. We provide a formative tool to strengthen your clarity of each process.

1. **Evidence:** This is the most important phase. The teacher and students co-construct success criteria based on the overarching learning intention. They need a crystal-clear understanding of quality expectations and evidence. Co-construction occurs through inquiry, teacher and student modeling, and the analysis of strong and weak work. The class uses the information to determine proficiency. Clear expectations allow for a body of evidence that reflects success criteria. It requires student engagement using accountable talk as they communicate their funds of knowledge.

**The Four-Step Co-Construction Process**
- Brainstorm the success criteria with students using examples and non-examples of student work.

- Students sort and organize the criteria into categories.
- Refine criteria with students.
- Create a rubric or checklist together.

2. **Analysis:** Students analyze their work through the lens of the success criteria. They use peer and self-assessment and reflections. They can work with a partner or the teacher. They use accountable talk to ensure authentic involvement instead of just being compliant. The talk involves scaffolding meaningful conversations that promote learning. Students must speak, listen, explain, confirm, extend, clarify, justify, and verbalize thoughts and opinions. They identify what they did well and what they need to work toward. Students think about thinking and compare their work to high-quality samples. They use work samples, learning progressions, checklists, and rubrics to support high-quality analysis. See the TAG protocol below for clarity in the process.

| T | A | G |
|---|---|---|
| **Talk about strengths:** | **Ask questions:** | **Give advice:** |
| • What were your strengths?<br>• What led to your success?<br>• I like how you _____<br>• I was impressed with _____<br>• _____ was a strength because _____ | • How did you get the idea for _____ ?<br>• What was your thinking behind _____?<br>• Can you help me understand _____?<br>• Can you clarify?<br>• What learning habits did you activate? | • May I give you some advice?<br>• What do you think your next step is?<br>• Have you thought about _____?<br>• I think focusing on _____ may help you improve. What do you think?<br>• This strategy worked for me. Do you want me to demonstrate? |

 **Tip 5.7**: Download and try this TAG asset-based peer feedback protocol.

3. **Action:** Students take action on the feedback they received. They revise their work and set short- and long-term goals. Partner with students to make goal setting cohesive and attached to the standards. Explain and model effective goal setting, and give students ample opportunities. Students must receive relevant feedback for forward propulsion purposes.

---

**Three Tips for Goal Setting**

**Offer students 1–3 months to noticeably improve. These three ways help students set goals (Gregory et al. 2011):**
- Break down general goals into manageable pieces.
- Model filling out planning frames goals.
- Have students interview one another about their goals to assist with clarification and revision (see below).

**Goal Setting Frame:**
- To make progress on _____, I could _____.
- How I plan to do this is _____.
- I will do this by _____.
- I can justify my success using the following evidence: _____.

**Peer Interview:**
- Can you accomplish your goal?
- How did you determine your time frame?
- How will you know you are progressing?
- What evidence will you use to justify your progress?
- Explain the models of success you used.
- Who can you collaborate with?

---

The A4L Classroom Protocol creates a learning cycle for students and teachers. Partnerships occur in each phase. The A4L protocol supports a deep implementation of formative assessment. Curricular goals and student needs determine the length of each cycle. Impact Teams ensure expectations and understanding, and they design learning cycles in incremental steps. Use the "Check-In" at the end of this chapter to self-assess your team and set refinement goals.

Note the importance of explaining and modeling each of the five practices of the formative assessment process with students. Thinking aloud models the thinking process. Teachers should model each component or use anonymous samples. Teachers gradually release responsibility to the students and provide constant feedback and coaching. This guarantees fidelity, reliability, and validity. Students must explicitly learn each component.

**A4L Classroom Protocol Template for Self- or Team Assessment**

| EVIDENCE | ANALYSIS | ACTION |
|---|---|---|
| • Communicate learning goals and co-construct success criteria using examples of student work<br>• Models applying success criteria to student work examples | • Provides quality peer and self-assessment models. Reflect so students can analyze their work and the work of peers<br>• Students practice peer and self-assessment<br>• Give students feedback on the quality of their assessments | • Students receive feedback and use it to revise and set goals<br>• Students monitor their goals with an accountability partner |

## Personal Reflection:

☐ How does your team consistently implement the core formative assessment practices with students?

☐ How can you make these practices more consistent?

# A4L Classroom Protocol Models of Success

Schools, teams, educators, and students experience mastery moments as they grow their expertise in the formative assessment process.

---

### Model of Success with Peer Review

### PS9, Naples Street Elementary, NYC DOE

As a PreK–5 in Staten Island, a school with two or three classes per grade level, consistency and vertical alignment is crucial. We brainstormed a common language that would make sense to students of all ages. We agreed on the stoplight system: Green—I got this; Yellow—I tried but needed some help, and Red—I needed help. We began using this system across all structures of the school day, including basic things such as lineup, cleanup, and playtime. What we found was surprising: Students as young as 4 years old were honest about their needs. The teachers quickly shifted the language into instruction by asking students to use the visual stoplight to self-assess after a mini-lesson and during independent work time. Again, students were reflective and truthful. Early on, students began to realize that it was acceptable to need help. They felt encouraged to express themselves when they did not understand something. Developing this trust with students set the tone for peer assessment.

Teachers began to create rubrics and checklists using standards-based success criteria, which provided clear expectations. We created a schoolwide template for success criteria using the stoplight system language to provide students with a familiar structure, format, and language across grade levels. We slowly began to model self-assessment with success criteria and exemplar pieces of work. We invited students to do the same. Our language was simple: "What did you do well?" and "What are your next steps?" We were amazed at how quickly students could identify their needs, and we saw a dramatic improvement in their work immediately. Admittedly, we went success criteria crazy!

Currently, we are focused on peer assessment. Using success criteria and flexible partnerships, students work together to provide one another with a "Glow" and a "Grow." A *glow* is a statement of positive feedback; a *grow* is the next step. Teachers co-constructed language stems to use when providing *glows and grows*. Peer assessment profoundly changed student work products. Our biggest discovery: student work remarkably improved when students received peer feedback.

My journey with self-and peer assessment began just about 7 years ago. This work transformed how my teachers plan for instruction and approach feedback. There is a level of trust among students and teachers that has inspired us to keep moving on this journey.

*Deanna Marco, Founding Principal, P.S. 9, Staten Island, New York*

**Personal Reflection:**

What did you learn from this model of success?

**Model of Success with Student Goal Setting**

**Lyons Township High School District, La Grange, IL**

 James Milkert, a former World History teacher from Lyons Township High School in Illinois, wanted to empower students to own their learning in his freshman-level class. He used the A4L Classroom Protocol to implement the formative assessment process with an emphasis on student goal setting.

Observe how James guides students to set goals. Notice the language James uses and his demeanor. View video 5.8 to see James in action.

**Personal Reflection:**

What did you learn from this model of success?

## Model of Success with Peer Feedback

## Tottenville High School, NYC DOE

**Puzzle of Practice:** While working with a high school team in N.Y., we identified peer feedback as an area of need and growth to support student agency and empowerment. The school tried peer feedback in the past with little success.

**Setting the Context:** Most teachers acknowledged that peer feedback could be powerful when it worked. But it took a lot of time and didn't work as effectively as they had hoped. Since we had a willing group of teachers, I introduced the Ladder of Feedback to them. In one of our Impact Team coaching sessions, we watched a video of a teacher using the ladder, and I demonstrated the microteaching protocol while the group watched. I showed how the process could look when building a consistent department practice.

**Steps to Success:** After watching the video and reviewing the steps for rolling out the Ladder of Feedback, we debriefed why peer feedback was not successful in the past. We identified some typical challenges when starting a student-led protocol and came up with solutions.

- The group agreed on a window of time to try out the protocol in an authentic and meaningful way. (This wasn't an add-on activity but; it aligned with the curriculum and theory of action.)
- Each teacher committed to teaching students how to use the Ladder of Feedback by modeling best practices and setting an environment conducive to students ownership. Teachers understood that this would be messy and take time.
- Students worked on each part of the ladder for multiple days. They submitted the work and a Ladder of Feedback graphic organizer.
- Teachers reviewed the documents and provided feedback.
- Teachers met as an Impact Team to discuss what they learned in the first round and made revisions.
- Teachers completed the whole process again.

**Our Impact:** The Impact Team used the Ladder of Feedback as a structure for enhancing student peer feedback. Students applied feedback success criteria, which improved student learning, particularly in the area of analysis. At first, only the Impact Team teachers worked on this protocol, but the practice spread. It became successfully employed in social studies and science classrooms. Teachers felt more confident about releasing control. Most importantly, with the Ladder of Feedback and standards-aligned formative assessment tasks, teachers successfully made better instructional choices to improve student achievement—for all demographics.

Author: Starr Sackstein, Impact Team Coach and *Hacking Assessment* author

**Personal Reflection:**

What did you learn from this model of success?

**Tip 5.8**: Starr is an author, blogger, and Core Collaborative Impact Team coach. She is committed to changing the way we do assessment, and you can read more in her most recent book, *Peer Feedback in the Classroom: Empowering Students to be the Experts.*

## LESSON STUDY PROTOCOL UNPACKED

Impact Teams use the Lesson Study Protocol to improve instructional effectiveness specific to formative assessment. Teacher teams examine their practice from the planning stage through teaching, observing, and critiquing during lesson studies. They create a detailed lesson plan. One teacher implements it while the others observe. The observation focuses on student responses. Based on the evidence, the team revises the lesson. The teachers reteach the lesson. See the online appendix for a detailed description of the Lesson Study Protocol and implementation rubric.

## Lesson Study Protocol Template

| EVIDENCE | ANALYSIS | ACTION |
|---|---|---|
| • Lesson plan<br>• Observation of lesson based on assessment data<br>• Take low inference notes<br>• Each person will have a different focus: engagement, clarity, etc.<br>• Focus on assets | • What was effective and why?<br>• What did you appreciate and why?<br>• What do you wonder about? | • What can we do collaboratively to improve this lesson?<br>• What are our next steps? |

### Model of Success with Peer Feedback

### Tottenville High School, NYC DOE

#### Puzzle of Practice

We struggle with building mathematics lessons that measure what teachers expect students to learn. Unfocused lessons are not as successful as intended, even when using backward design and learning intentions to establish assessment criteria.

#### The Solution

After creating a lesson for a specific group of students (and much articulation about intentions and measuring progress), teachers needed help communicating the goals. We would plan, but it simply failed.

• This year, we built learning intentions into the lesson plan *and* success criteria. (This was the missing piece.)
• As the lesson development progressed, we referred back to the unpacked learning intentions and success criteria to stay on track.
• The learning intentions and success criteria table explicitly explained the goals to students.

## Our Impact

Teachers communicate the learning, and students have a better idea of what they should be learning. That streamlines focus, and student exit cards showed better conceptual understanding.

The example below came from a group of high school freshman teachers concerned with gaps. The associated lesson comes from a set of lessons that includes *number talks* and *close reading* taught during the first 2 weeks of school.

## Learning Intentions:

- *Describe the distributive property in your own words*
- *Give an example of the distributive property*
- *Write and solve a numerical expression (distributive property) from a contextual situation*
- *Change numeric expression to algebraic expression and solve*

## Success Criteria

- *Accurately describe the distributive property as "multiplying everything inside the ( ) by the number outside."*
- *Provide contextual (preferred) or numerical expression (acceptable)*
- *$2(\$5 + \$3) = \$16$*
- *Represent a word problem as a numerical expression and solve $2(x + 3) = 16$*
- *Change a numerical expression to an algebraic expression and solve*

**Author:** Carol Cronk, Impact Team Coach, Victorville, CA

## Team Reflection:

☐ How would your team use the EAA Lesson Study Protocol to work through a puzzle of practice regarding formative assessment?

☐ What formative practice would your team focus on to engage in a lesson study? (Co-construction of success criteria, feedback, accountable talk, self- and peer assessment, reflection, questioning, goal setting?)

## MICROTEACHING UNPACKED

When a team of teachers sets out to improve, refine, or implement a pedagogical practice, they use the Microteaching Protocol. They engage in a video review of lessons or small parts of lessons. They share feedback about improving or adapting the practice. They record mini-lessons based on a strategy or approach before the Impact Team meetings, typically when using the Analysis of Evidence (AOE) Protocol. The team observes the video and provides feedback to the creator. Each team member tries the technique, and the group summarizes the session. Please see the online appendix for a detailed EAA Microteaching Protocol and implementation rubric description.

### Microteaching Protocol Template

| EVIDENCE | ANALYSIS | ACTION | |
|---|---|---|---|
| • Video observation<br>• Take low inference notes<br>• Focus on assets | • What was effective and why?<br>• What did you appreciate and why?<br>• What do you wonder about? | • How might we adapt or try this in our classroom? | |

**Tip 5.9:** You can learn more about micro-teaching from the Center for Innovative Teaching and Learning at Northern Illinois University.

# Model of Success Example 1

| Micro-Teaching Model of Success: Launching Peer Review |
| Lyons Township High School District, La Grange, IL |

The Social Studies team wanted to build capacity in peer and self-assessment. The American Studies lead teacher, Virginia Condon, volunteered to engage in a coaching cycle to ensure there were  quality think-aloud models and the role of student work samples in peer assessment.

Virginia recorded herself guiding students with peer review in her class. The team observed the video and analyzed it to determine strengths and possible next steps for using the strategy. They practiced with a colleague before teaching it to their students.

## PHASE ONE:  EVIDENCE

**Peer Facilitator:** Today, we observed Virginia Condon model the Ladder of Feedback with her American Studies class. *She used the think-aloud strategy to model the Ladder of Feedback Protocol for her students, and then the students tried it on their own with their essay introductions. Virginia modeled these three steps:*

- *Value*
- *Clarify*
- *Suggestions*

## PHASE TWO: ANALYSIS

**Peer Facilitator:** After observing the video, what was effective? Why? Do you have any questions or wonderings?

**Team Shares:**
- The think-aloud was very clear.
- The students thought the Ladder of Feedback was effective; they could use the model to support the process.
- The template offered helpful sentence stems.
- The students engaged in filling out a blank template.
- Would you continue to use this approach? Why? What would you change if you did it again?

**Virginia:** Yes, the template worked well. I broke up the process and allowed students to talk more. I really appreciated the positive feedback.

**PHASE THREE: ACTION**

**Peer Facilitator:** How would you turnkey this approach in your classroom? How would you adapt it to fit your students' needs?

· *Each teacher shared adaptation ideas for their curriculum with a partner. They also did so in teams.*

**Peer Facilitator: What did we learn?**

· *Think-aloud is very important when teaching peer review. We need to model each step and not assume the students know what to do. Breaking the process into smaller chunks makes sense when ensuring a high-quality process.*

**Note:** See videos 5.9 and 5.10 at the end of this chapter to observe peer feedback in action.

# NUTSHELL

Accountable talk and reflection infuse the formative process throughout the five core formative assessment practices. We develop a learning-focused relationship when we involve students in all aspects of the formative assessment process—in partnership with each other and the teacher. Partnering with students balances traditional power structures and strengthens relational trust. Implementing formative assessment uses pedagogies that strengthen efficacy, collaborative learning, goal setting, peer and self-assessment, reflection, and using exemplars or models of success to co-construct success criteria.

The A4L Classroom Protocol gives teacher teams a formative assessment process roadmap. Teams use the Lesson Study, Peer Coaching, and Microteaching Protocols to refine formative practices and advance pedagogical expertise. Quality formative assessment provides a learning framework for effective teaching and learning.

## Team Reflection:

What is the A4L Classroom Protocol and why is at the heart of the Impact Team Model?

How does the A4L Classroom Protocol align with your teacher evaluation system or professional teaching standards?

What is the state of "assessment for learning" in your system?

What evidence do you have that suggests this?

How would your team use *Microteaching, Peer Coaching* and *Lesson Study* to refine implementation of the formative practices?

What formative assessment practices would you refine?

## Equity Reflection:

What do you notice and wonder about different student group experiences with formative assessment?

How do we support students in using diverse languages and communication styles?

How do we ensure that all students have agency over their learning?

## CHECK-IN

Use the rubric to assess the quality of formative assessment in your school or classroom. Use evidence to justify your reasoning. Then determine a collaborative inquiry team goal based on your assessment.

| EVIDENCE | Not Yet | Sometimes | Always |
|---|---|---|---|
| **Communicating learning intentions and co-constructing success criteria** | | | |
| Students articulate the learning intention and speak to relevance. | | | |
| Students reflect and discuss the essential question(s) and big ideas throughout the learning cycle. | | | |
| We use exemplars, examples and non-examples, and think-alouds to co-construct success criteria with students. | | | |
| Learners identify success criteria in student work samples. | | | |
| Learners use student work samples, rubrics, checklists, and learning progressions to guide their learning. | | | |
| What's next? | | | |

| ANALYSIS | Not Yet | Sometimes | Always |
|---|---|---|---|
| **Self- and peer assessment and reflection** | | | |
| Model peer and self-assessment using student work samples. Think aloud while modeling. | | | |
| Model respectfully giving and receiving evidence-based feedback. Post feedback language stems and frames for students. | | | |

| | Not Yet | Sometimes | Always |
|---|---|---|---|
| Students use rubrics and checklists to engage in self-assessment and peer assessment. | | | |
| Students get regular practice applying the success criteria. | | | |
| Students identify success criteria in each other's work. | | | |
| Students respectfully give and receive feedback using success criteria and accountable talk. | | | |
| Students receive regular teacher feedback to lift the quality and accuracy of their assessments. | | | |
| What's next? | | | |

| ACTION | Not Yet | Sometimes | Always |
|---|---|---|---|
| **Revision, goal setting and monitoring** | | | |
| Students reflect on their strengths and next steps based on teacher, peer, and self- assessment. | | | |
| Models using the feedback to revise. | | | |
| Use evidence-based feedback to model setting personal learning goals and action plans. | | | |
| Students create personal learning goals based on feedback from peer and self-assessments. | | | |
| Students track their mastery of focus standards progress and organize their progress. | | | |
| What's next? | | | |

## Activity:

Leverage the four sources of efficacy by engaging students regularly in the formative assessment process. How do formative practices align with the four sources of efficacy? Use the table below and the list of formative assessment practices to organize your thinking.

Formative Practices: (1) communicating learning intentions, (2) co-constructing success criteria with samples of student work, (3) accountable talk, (4) reflection, (5) questioning, (6) self-and peer assessment, (7) revision, (8) goal setting and monitoring, (9) learning from mistakes, and (10) ensuring empathy/compassion when giving feedback.

| Four Sources of Efficacy | Classroom Examples | |
|---|---|---|
| Mastery Moments | *Example: Master a personal learning goal* | |
| Learning Vicariously Through Models of Success | *Example: Using exemplars to co-construct success criteria* | |
| Feedback or Verbal Persuasion | | |
| Safety | | |

**Mastery Moments: Video Descriptions**

**Chapter 5: Strengthening Student Efficacy: The Formative Assessment Process in Action**

Overview: The videos in this chapter illustrate the A4L Classroom Protocol. We developed the protocol to guide teacher learning teams and instructional leaders. All of the videos took place during instructional time.

Impact Teams use videos to scale up formative assessment expertise using our Lesson Study and Microteaching Protocols.

| | |
|---|---|
| | **Video 5.5:** Peer and Self-assessment: Writer's Workshop, Kindergarten, P.S. 45, District 31, New York City DOE |
| | **Video 5.6:** Observe self and peer assessment practices in elementary classrooms. Mathematics, Seventh Grade, IS 34, District 31, New York City DOE |
| | **Video 5.7:** Scaffolding Peer Assessment: Ninth-Grade World History, Lyons Township High School (LTHS), La Grange, Illinois |
| | **Video 5.8:** Scaffolding Goal Setting: Ninth-Grade World History, LTHS, La Grange, Illinois |
| | **Video 5.9:** Modeling the Ladder of Feedback: American Studies, LTHS, La Grange, Illinois |

| | |
|---|---|
| | **Video 5.10:** Feedback on Feedback: American Studies, High School, LTHS, La Grange, Illinois |
| | **Video 5.11:** Feedback on Feedback: Chemistry, 11th Grade, LTHS, La Grange, Illinois |
| | **Video 5.12:** Student-Led Small Group Teaching, P.S. 60, District 31, NYC DOE |
| | **Video 5.13:**<br>Observe secondary students in action with self and peer assessment in this YouTube playlist featuring our partner schools. |
| | **Video 5.14:**<br>Observe students during the goal setting process in this YouTube playlist featuring our partner schools. |
| | **Video 5.15:**<br>Observe students engaging in reflection in this YouTube playlist featuring our partner schools. |

When students have consistent opportunities to develop their ability to self- and peer assess and reflect, they learn more about themselves as learners and each other.

Bloomberg et al., 2022, p. 186

# EQUITABLE, VIABLE, AND COHERENT CURRICULUM

## CREATING CONTEXT FOR EFFICACY

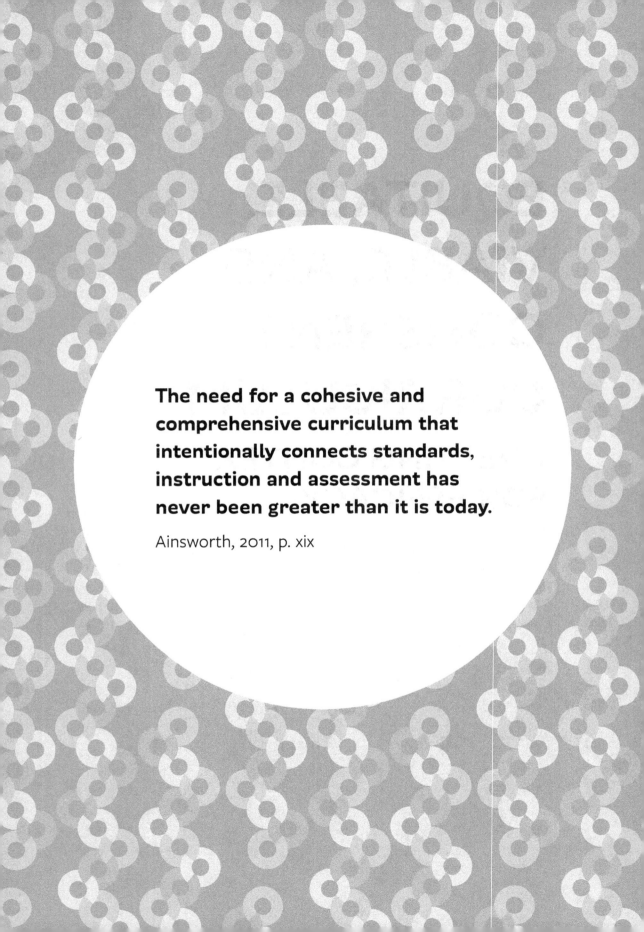

**The need for a cohesive and comprehensive curriculum that intentionally connects standards, instruction and assessment has never been greater than it is today.**

Ainsworth, 2011, p. xix

## Mastery Moment

What strengths does your team employ to create clear, culturally responsive and sustaining learning pathways?

# THE *WHAT:* EQUITY, VIABILITY, AND COHERENCE

Strengthening student efficacy requires systems to provide an *equitable, viable,* and *coherent* (EVC) curriculum. The curriculum provides a context for learning and is the first step in building a learning environment that strengthens efficacy. A quality learning environment coupled with evidence-based teaching methods can improve self-efficacy (Bandura, 1994). Quality curriculum doesn't just communicate the *what* to teachers, it also directs the *how.*

Effective curriculums create time and space for students to participate in formative assessment core practices that strengthen efficacy beliefs. We want students to own learning and master standards that transfer across content areas, college, and careers. Self-empowered learners learn for themselves, give and receive feedback, set and monitor goals, and work collaboratively.

As educators address the challenge of helping *all* students master state standards, one element has been identified as a key to successful school improvement efforts—that is, aligning what we assess with what we teach. With the advent of next-generation standards, school districts nationwide strive to build the capacity to strengthen teaching and learning. Districts, schools, and regional centers involve teachers across the system to personalize overarching K–12 curriculum resources. We need to align the written, taught, and tested curricula to what their students actually need. We have determined three factors that serve as lenses for designing or revising curriculum documents to keep students at the center of the learning and ensure fidelity of the formative assessment process:

1. Equity.

2. Viability

3. Coherence

## EQUITY

An equitable curriculum has two dimensions. The first is *inclusion*— ensuring that all students have access to *relevant* learning aligned with state standards. It seems obvious, but students need the opportunity to learn the content. Marzano (2003) indicated a discrepancy between intended and implemented curricula. Classroom learning does not necessarily align with district expectations, and this discrepancy prohibits students from attaining the intended curriculum. Teachers must collaboratively unpack what they plan and create a common understanding of learning intentions. Then there is a need to communicate intentions to students in a digestible way; they can't take ownership of requirements they do not understand. When teachers and students understand the expectations, the learning speed can double (Hattie, 2009).

The second dimension is *fairness*: making sure that personal and social circumstances—for example, gender, socio-economic status, or ethnic origin—do not stand in the way of educational potential (OECD, 2008). We subscribe to the notion that *fairness isn't equal.* *Fair isn't Equal* was introduced to the education community in 1988 by Allen Mendler and David Yellen. So, what is a fair curriculum? Many define it as teaching everyone the same curriculum simultaneously, adhering to a strict pacing guide or a textbook, and using summative assessment to rank, sort, grade, and categorize students.

It focuses on what the teacher teaches, not what the students learn. Doing so is the most unfair way to treat students. This practice harms students.

Students are not all the same (thank goodness). They have different motivations, cultural backgrounds, needs, and learning goals. However, our ultimate mission remains the same: advancing learner agency. An equitable curriculum honors and values the needs of our learners by adopting asset-based pedagogies that override the deficit-based models that plague our current system. The California Department of Education (2022) explains that "asset-based pedagogies view the diversity that students bring to the classroom, including culture, language, disability, socio-economic status, immigration status, and sexuality as characteristics that add value and strength to classrooms and communities" (para. 1).

In her book *Cultivating Genius*, Dr. Gholdy E. Muhammad (2020) presents a four-layered equity framework—one that is grounded in history. It restores excellence to curriculum and instruction. This framework, which she names "Historically Responsive Literacy," is essential and universal for all students, especially youth of color, who traditionally have been marginalized by learning standards, school policies, and classroom practices. Her curricular equity framework helps educators teach and lead toward the following pursuits:

- Identity development—making sense of themselves and others
- Skill development—developing proficiencies across academic disciplines
- Intellectual development—gaining knowledge and becoming smarter
- Criticality—developing the ability to read print and social contexts concerning power, equity, and oppression

All students receive profound personal, intellectual, and academic success opportunities when these four learning pursuits come together through her Historically Responsive Literacy framework.

 **Tip 6.1**: Build connection and rapport by using these questions from the National Equity Project to support identity development.

An equitable curriculum creates time and space for formative assessment to flourish, offering ample time for students to peer and self-assess. It includes time for feedback aligned with success criteria. It offers time for revision and goal setting. It allows students to reflect on learning and grow from their mistakes. The assessment framework described in *Amplify Learner Voice through Culturally Responsive and Sustaining Assessment* honors the cultural identity of learners by reimagining formative assessment through an asset-based, culturally responsive lens (Bloomberg et al., 2023). It infuses seven core concepts into experience : (1) cultural identity, (2) asset-centered mindset, (3) habits of learning, (4) learning partnerships, (5) learner clarity, (6) authentic engagement, and (7) criticality.

## VIABILITY

Time is a major consideration when determining critical focus areas for curriculum documents. You can only attain a viable curriculum if given time (Marzano, 2003). Teachers need adequate instructional time. Unfortunately, the typical school year has too many standards to teach and learn. We prioritize state standards so students learn and master essential skills and concepts.

We advocate prioritizing transferable standards students can use across content areas, college, and careers. We call them *focus standards*. Teachers assess focus standards using formative assessment with students. They delineate and communicate them on curriculum maps to keep the system on the same page. Rubrics and scoring guides support focus standards so students can monitor their learning based on the success criteria. Students must engage in deliberate or goal-directed practice over time (Bloomberg et al., 2022). All stakeholders regularly monitor and celebrate mastery progress using the essential standards of goal setting, learning portfolios, student-led conferences, exhibitions of learning, and e-portfolios.

## COHERENCE

Curriculum coherence conceptualizes the big ideas in each course, grade level, and content area. It builds ideas across time and disciplines, connecting relevant topics and aligning instruction. The term *coherent curriculum*, or aligned curriculum, refers to an academic program that is:

(1) well organized and purposefully designed to facilitate learning

(2) free of academic gaps and needless repetitions

(3) aligned across lessons, courses, subject areas, and grade levels.

The foundation of a coherent curriculum is built upon learning intentions (or targets). Big ideas come from focus standards and create learning intention relevance, ensuring intra- and inter-unit coherence. Intra-unit coherence focuses on a few key big ideas rather than superficially covering many unrelated ideas. Inter-unit coherence addresses those same big ideas in multiple units within and across disciplines. Students construct integrated knowledge across units and years.

We must develop learning progressions or pathways from each unit's focus standards and intentions to support inter- and intra-unit coherence. Learning progressions represent the subgoals of the ultimate learning intention and standard. Present learning progressions to students as a continuum of learning, accounting for different learning rates (DeMeester and Jones 2009). Individual student's progress will vary along the learning path, but progressions should connect knowledge, concepts, and skills students develop as they evolve from novices to experts (Heritage, 2008).

 **Tip 6.2**: Visit the online appendix for more learning progression examples.

# THE NEED FOR MULTI-TIERED SYSTEMS OF SUPPORT

Systems matter. Consider the quality of core instruction our students need. Rethink the role of curriculum in a larger context. It is vital to student success. MTSS (multi-tiered systems of support) give educators this context. MTSS is an integrated, comprehensive learning framework focused on:

- quality core instruction aligned to next-generation standards
- differentiated and personalized instruction
- student-centered learning
- aligned systems necessary for all learners' academic, behavioral, and social/emotional success

The Core Collaborative Learning Network, devoted to advancing learning agencies for the past decade and home of the ITM, envisioned an intentional human-centered design MTSS framework. The framework guides teams in developing solutions to challenges by involving the human perspective in all steps of the problem-solving process. Impact Teams integrate five MTSS core components (see Figure 6.1) for an integrated, comprehensive framework focused on:

1. A balanced assessment framework
2. High-impact, differentiated instruction aligned to the Universal Design for Learning (UDL) framework
3. Culturally responsive supports and resources
4. Restorative support and relational literacy
5. Community-based support

MTSS creates needed systemic change through intentional design (and redesign) of services. It quickly identifies supports to match the needs of all students. The California Department of Education (2022) explains the scope of MTSS, including:

- aligning all initiatives, supports, and resources with an equitable, viable, and coherent curriculum
- systematically addressing support for all students

**Figure 6.1: Impact Teams MTSS Core Components**

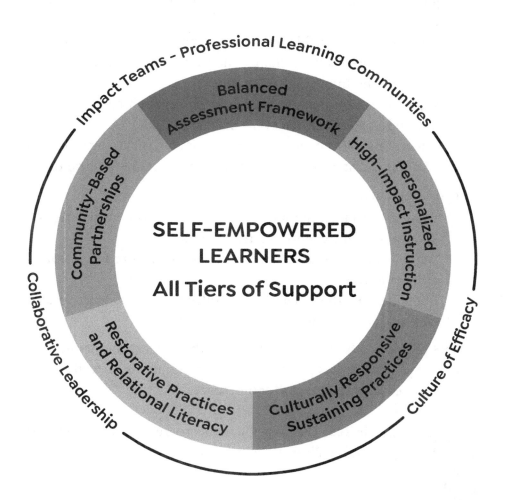

Learn more about
the *Impact Teams*
*MTSS* model.

- endorsing Universal Design for Learning instructional strategies, giving all students differentiated content, process, and products
- integrating sustainable instructional and intervention support
- inviting school staff to change the traditional systems by adopting the Impact Team Model
- supporting high-quality standards and research-based culturally and linguistically relevant instruction
- integrating data collection and assessment, including universal screening, diagnostics, and progress monitoring for each tier

We also included:

- using EAA to identify practice puzzles, develop interventions, and evaluate intervention effectiveness
- school wide positive behavioral supports anchored in restorative practices
- implementing the Impact Team collaborative approach to data analysis, co-construction, and intervention

MTSS provides a basis for partnering with students and families to ensure equitable access to next-generation standards, as well as core social and emotional learning competencies.

 **Tip 6.3**: Use the QR code to read more about the Impact Team MTSS model.

# THE *WHY*: RESEARCH AND REASONS

## REASON 1: THE QUALITY OF THE CURRICULUM IMPACTS EQUITY.

All students must be able to learn the curriculum's critical content (Marzano, 2012). However, the curriculum leaves too many students out in various ways: long-standing opportunity gaps, mobility, lack of coherence or clarity, and textbook-dominated curriculums devoid of standards and culturally responsive and sustaining education practices.

## REASON 2: WELL-PLANNED CURRICULUM ENABLES STUDENTS TO DEVELOP EFFICACY.

Quality learning environments and teaching methods improve self-efficacy (Bandura, 1994). Use the following pedagogies.

- Cooperative learning structures. Students promote positive self-evaluations of capability and academics with one another (Bandura, 1994).
- Establish specific, challenging, *attainable* short-term goals (Schunk & Pajares, 2002).
- Help students lay out a specific learning strategy and verbalize their plans. As students proceed, ask them to note their progress and verbalize their next steps.
- Compare student performance to their goals, not another student or the rest of the class (Bandura, 1994).

## REASON 3: CLEARLY DEFINED LEARNING PROGRESSIONS CREATE ACCESS TO CONTENT.

Students may need to gain prerequisite skills and knowledge to successfully master grade-level standard(s). Learning progressions serve as entry points and pathways. They are important to developing progressive sophistication in skills within a domain (Heritage et al. 2009).

## REASON 4: TEACHER CLARITY IMPACTS STUDENT LEARNING.

Teachers must communicate the intentions of the lessons and success criteria. Clear descriptions include skills, knowledge, attitudes, and values. Teachers need to know their lessons' goals and success criteria, student progressions, and know where to go next. Teacher clarity has a .84 effect size on student learning, doubling the learning speed for students (Hattie, 2023).

## REASON 5: CAREFULLY CRAFTED CURRICULUM ENABLES LEARNING TRANSFER.

For students to succeed in college and careers, we must emphasize learning transfer: the application of skills, knowledge, and attitudes from one experience to a new context (Perkins & Salomon, 1992). Therefore, to produce positive learning transfers, we need to practice learning in various contexts. Rigorous PBL supports learning transfer at all levels of rigor (surface-deep-transfer).

# THE *HOW*: SIX CURRICULAR STEPS FOR SUCCESS

Creating an equitable, viable, coherent curriculum takes time and requires collaboration at all system levels. The following six steps guide necessary actions to revise or develop optimal conditions for learning.

## STEP 1: DETERMINE FOCUS STANDARDS

Identify and communicate the essential content for all students. Use vertical Impact Teams at the elementary level and in departmental Impact Teams at the secondary level. Select focus standards to create coherence across the curriculum. Clearly delineate essential vs. unessential content. Teams may use the lenses, listed below and illustrated in Figure 6.2, to choose focus standards.

- Are the prospective focus standards transferable across content areas?
- Are the standards transferable to college, career, and life?
- Does existing data show a need for prioritized focus standards?
- Are the prospective focus standards crucial? How many years will students need to master them?

**Figure 6.2 Determining Focus Standards**

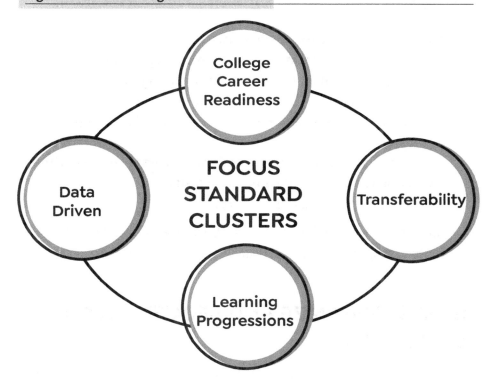

## STEP 2: DETERMINE REQUIRED TIME

*All* students need focus standards. During curriculum mapping, the Impact Team should estimate the instructional time needed for the focus standards skills and concepts (English, 2010; Marzano et al., 1999). Dedicate time to

- teaching—explaining, modeling, guided practice, inquiry, and feedback
- learning—deliberate practice, peer and self-assessment, feedback, revision, goal setting, and reflections

# STEP 3: UNPACK FOR CLARITY

This protocol familiarizes teams with the standards, learning outcomes, and educational methods and allows for partnering with students. It engages teams in

- researching a cluster of standards
- identifying key learning progression concepts and skills
- shaping overarching learning intentions (big ideas and essential questions)
- defining competencies at all rigor levels (surface, deep, and transfer)
- determining surface-, deep-, and transfer-level success criteria
- creating formative and summative tasks
- aligning focus standards resources

*Special thanks to Dr. Michael McDowell, Kara Vandas, and Isaac Wells for contributing to the revised Unpacking for Clarity Protocol.*

# STEP 4: ORGANIZE AND SEQUENCE FOR COHERENCE

Consider the following when placing focus standards into units of study.

- Introduce more cognitively demanding focus standards earlier to offer many opportunities to succeed. (Hint: Depth of knowledge (DOK) helps to determine the time needed for mastery.)
- The curriculum document directs teachers to teach these standards explicitly toward the beginning of the year.

- Focus standards should repeat across units, giving students multiple opportunities.
- Strategically place supporting standards to support focus standards.

## STEP 5: CELEBRATE PROGRESS

Teachers and students monitor and celebrate mastery focus progress.
- Schedule learning celebrations (student-led conferences, goal-setting assemblies, exhibitions of learning, and e-portfolios)
- Invite families and caregivers to support event planning. Offer options for celebration engagement (virtual, at different times of the day for families, etc.).

## STEP 6: REENGAGE FOR EQUITY WITH MTSS

Fair isn't equal! Students are different. They do not learn at the same rate, and they all start in different places. Many times, this is due to long-standing opportunity gaps that have been built into our deficit-minded system for decades. As explained earlier, the MTSS framework disrupts inequitable systems by systematically focusing on all students.
- improve academics and social-emotional behavior outcomes
- address unmet needs
- de-silo data and make systems interconnected and more effective
- adopt a whole-child approach to supporting learners
- help students become empowered learners—no matter where they start

Students have all year to master focus standards. Allot time inside each subsequent unit and core instructional time for re-engagement at all rigor levels. Schools and districts innovatively find extra re-engagement time within Tier 1 core instruction. Some schools add 3 to 5 days after the unit summative assessment for designated Tier 1 peer tutoring, 1:1 coaching, and small group support. Other schools create asynchronous, deliberate practice opportunities using programs like i-Ready or Zearn.

## Tier 2 and Tier 3 support:

Allot extra time during the school day (and outside of it) for students who need Tier 2 and Tier 3 support. Deliberately practice prerequisite skills at all rigor levels. Some schools designate time for Tier 2 and Tier 3 re-engagement or WIN Time (*what I need*) each day, in addition to quality Tier 1. differentiation. Regardless of the context and support tier, prioritize the following:

- allot time to self-assess, peer assess, reflect, and monitor individual learning goals.
- opportunities for goal-directed, deliberate practice and feedback
- progress-monitoring using the Analysis of Evidence (AOE) Protocol throughout the learning cycle
- collective action that support students' journeys toward proficiency

Consider differentiating the formative task so all learners have access. If your team already knows how students will perform the task before you give it, you are not gaining information. Formative assessment looks for bright spots. Use learning progression to differentiate tasks on a path for progress, ensuring that students get exactly what they need.

## Implement an Equitable, Viable, and Coherent Curriculum

Implementing an equitable, viable, and coherent curriculum has inherent benefits for strengthening student efficacy. Table 6.1 outlines key curricular practices that strengthen efficacy.

**Table 6.1: The Do's and Don'ts of an Equitable-Viable-Coherent Curriculum**

| Do | Don't |
|---|---|
| • Ensure a clear understanding of learning intentions and success criteria (clarity)<br>• Adopt asset-based pedagogies to ensure students feel valued and affirmed (safety)<br>• Give multiple opportunities for success (mastery moments)<br>• Guide students to set relevant short- and long-term goals<br>• Create opportunities for regular collaboration (safety)<br>• Provide exemplars (models of success)<br>• Create regular opportunities for peer and self-assessment (feedback)<br>• Ensure that Tier 2 and Tier 3 support engages students at all levels of rigor<br>• Infuse habits of learning into all tiers of support<br>• Infuse SEL experiences into the learning experiences<br>• Foster an equitable and positive school culture by restoratively strengthening connections between youth and adults | • Implement inflexible "lock-step" instruction: a formulaic setting makes it harder for students to ask questions or become involved (Bandura, 1994)<br>• Use only whole group instruction or lecture approaches as a vehicle for teaching and learning<br>• Teach textbooks with fidelity. Teachers must personalize standards-based instruction to meet student needs<br>• Implement teaching practices that compare students' performance against each other—this may raise the self-efficacy of the top students, but it will lower the self-efficacy of the rest of the class (Bandura, 1994)<br>• Make what is taught more important than what students learn<br>• Water down Tier 2 and Tier 3 support by engaging students in only surface-level learning<br>• Grade students when they are engaged in deliberate practice; students need specific feedback, but grades do not offer quality feedback<br>• Use deficit-based disciplinary approaches that harm students |

**Tip 6.4**: Rigorous PBL viably closes opportunity gaps. *The Project Habit*, by Michael McDowell and Kelley Miller, describes 15 small shifts for busy teachers looking to enhance and innovate their practices. The shifts aim to ensure students establish agency, develop rigorous academic content knowledge and skills, and apply that learning to real-world problems. Use this QR code to access the 15 habits.

## Unpacking for Clarity Unpacked

Teachers often use the Unpacking for Clarity Protocol when working toward curricular goals. This protocol helps teams learn the standards, develop quality formative and summative tasks to gather student evidence, determine instructional strategies at all rigor levels (surface-deep-transfer), and align instructional resources. Unpacking for Clarity keeps everyone on the same page. It allows teams to partner with students in formative assessment. It engages teams in

1. Researching the focus standards cluster
2. Defining key concepts and skills by framing the learning progression
3. Determining overarching learning intentions with essential questions and big ideas
4. Developing success criteria or key competencies at all rigor levels
5. Using engagement strategies at all rigor levels
6. Building criterion-based formative and summative assessment tasks
7. Infusing habits of learning to support "learning how to learn"
8. Aligning evidence-based resources to the focus standards cluster

Unpack collaboratively to ensure alignment between teaching and assessment. The protocol focuses on conversation and dialogue. Many teams gain clarity by charting their thinking on posters or docs. You can use the below template as a note-catcher to memorialize the team's thinking.

 **Tip 6.5**: Additional examples of Unpacking for Clarity across content areas can be found in the online appendix.

## Designing an Equitable, Viable, and Coherent Curriculum

| Model of Success: Deliberate Practice<br>Hugo Newman School (PS-IS 180), Harlem, NYC DOE | |
| --- | --- |
|  | **Video 6.1**: Former K-8 principal, Jeneca Parker, discusses the role of deliberate practice for mastery learning. During the 2022-2023 school year, the school's impact teams developed more curricular coherence, giving students more time to deliberately practice standards' expertise. This practice integrates reflection and self-assessment into the process. |

| Model of Success with the Impact Team MTSS Model<br>Amistad Elementary, Kennewick, WA | |
| --- | --- |
|  | **Video 6.2:** Former reading specialist Rhonda MacLellan shows how Amistad Elementary Impact Teams created a new master schedule centered around students. They offered more deliberate practice time for English Language development, resulting in a positive impact. The school reclassified more multilingual learners than they ever had before and led the district in reclassification rates. |
| | K-5 Impact Teams differentiated systematic instruction in phonemic awareness, phonics, and sight words for all readers. This targeted differentiation for core instruction created a positive impact. The school met its growth goal for these learners. Fifty percent more students developed reading foundational skills expertise. |

**Model of Success: Designing an Equitable, Viable, Coherent Curriculum**
**Naples Street Elementary (PS9) Impact Team Leaders, NYC DOE**

**Video 6.3**: Learn from teacher leaders, Graziela Casale and Lauren Stasio, from PS 9 in Staten Island, NY. They constantly evolve their curriculum to meet student needs. Most recently, they have adopted asset-based culturally responsive and sustaining education practices with Dr. Ingrid Tyman. They learned how to maximize cultural assets as a source of knowledge. Learn how this work changed their perception of teaching and learning.

**Model of Success: Designing Equitable, Viable and Coherent Curriculum**
**Park Middle School, Kennewick, WA**

**Video 6.4:** Learn from Gina Ferguson, Park Middle instructional coach, about her school's journey when designing an equitable, viable, and coherent curriculum to ensure student agency. Curricular coherence ensures that students have more time to practice key priority standards and peer and self-assess.

# NUTSHELL

An equitable, viable, and coherent curriculum creates the context for implementing formative assessment. Three factors serve as lenses for designing or revising curriculum documents to keep students at the center of learning with fidelity.

1. Equity

2. Viability

3. Coherence

*Unpacking for Clarity* helps teacher teams ensure curricular clarity and consistency, providing a context for learning. It is the first step to building a learning environment that strengthens efficacy.

## Team Reflection:

☐  Why is clarity important for learners?

☐  How do you know your team members are clear about expectations?

☐  How do you ensure clarity of curricular expectations with students?

☐  How do you balance student needs with curricular goals?

## Equity Reflection:

☐  How does our curriculum provide all students opportunities to leverage diverse assets?

☐  How does our curriculum provide mirrors and windows for children to explore themselves and diverse perspectives?

# CHECK-IN

Assess your curriculum for equity, viability, and coherence with the below checklist. Determine the next steps based on your results.

| Action Steps | Not Yet | In Progress | Next Steps |
|---|---|---|---|
| **Step 1: Determine Focus Standards** | | | |
| Are the prospective focus standards transferable across content areas? | | | |
| Are the standards transferable to college, career, and life? | | | |
| Does existing data show a need for prioritized focus standards? | | | |

| Action Steps | Not Yet | In Progress | Next Steps |
|---|---|---|---|
| **Step 1: Determine Focus Standards, continued** | | | |
| Are the prospective focus standards crucial? How many years will students need to master them? | | | |
| **Step 2: Determine Time Needed** | | | |
| Teaching: Explaining, modeling, guided practice, inquiry, and feedback | | | |
| Learning: Deliberate and spaced practice, peer and self-assessment, feedback, revision, goal setting, reflection, and learning from mistakes | | | |
| **Step 3: Unpack for Clarity** | | | |
| Research the standard. | | | |
| Determine the learning progression. | | | |
| Determine transferable, overarching big ideas and essential questions. | | | |
| Develop success criteria at all levels of rigor (surface, deep, and transfer). | | | |
| Determine strategies at all rigor levels. | | | |
| Design formative and summative tasks at all levels of rigor (surface-deep-transfer). | | | |

| Action Steps | Not Yet | In Progress | Next Steps |
|---|---|---|---|
| **Step 3: Unpack for Clarity, continued** | | | |
| Align evidence-based resources to focus standard clusters. | | | |
| **Step 4: Organize and Sequence for Coherence** | | | |
| Introduce more cognitively demanding focus standards earlier to offer many opportunities to succeed. | | | |
| The curriculum document directs teachers to teach these standards explicitly toward the beginning of the year. | | | |
| Focus standards should repeat across units, giving students multiple opportunities to succeed. | | | |
| Strategically place supporting standards to support focus standards. | | | |
| **Step 5: Celebrate Progress** | | | |
| Schedule learning celebrations (student-led conferences, goal-setting assemblies, exhibitions of learning, and e-portfolios). | | | |
| Invite families and caregivers to support event planning. Offer options for celebration engagement (virtual, at different times of the day, etc.). | | | |

| Action Steps | Not Yet | In Progress | Next Steps |
|---|---|---|---|
| **Step 6: Reengage for Equity with MTSS** | | | |
| Students monitor individual learning goals. | | | |
| Provide deliberate practice opportunities during Tier 1 core instruction to reengage students. | | | |
| Provide Tier 2 and Tier 3 supports as needed. | | | |
| Support students at all levels of rigor (surface, deep, and transfer) across all tiers of support and learning habits are infused. | | | |
| Progress monitor to ensure positive impacts. | | | |

As you use this checklist on existing curricular documents, conduct a greater curriculum audit. Ensure that it is culturally responsive and sustainable.

 **Tip 6.6**: The NYU Metro Center designed the Culturally Responsive English Language Arts Curriculum Scorecard to assess their school's ELA curriculum. You can access the scorecard using this QR code.

## Collective Action:

1. Based on your curriculum assessment, what are your strengths?

2. Based on your curriculum assessment, what are your next curriculum revision steps?

3. What is the revision timeline?

# EVIDENCE TO INFORM AND ACT

Learning from evidence requires a deeply personal appreciation of how it is essential to one's professional learning and growth. Without such appreciation and the associated skills, data use becomes an exercise in evaluating other people rather than in collective learning and improvement.

Robinson, 2011

### Mastery Moment

Think of a time when your team successfully used evidence to make decisions about teaching and learning.

# THE *WHAT*: USING QUALITY EVIDENCE TO INFORM AND ACT

The best-selling business book *In Search of Excellence* (Peters & Waterman, 1982) first used *"data rich and information poor* (DRIP)" to describe organizations lacking meaningful information. We now live in a world where immense amounts of data are exploding exponentially every day. Unfortunately, there isn't a practical way to analyze this expansive amount of data. The "DRIP" phenomena makes organizations data rich and information poor. Our schools and districts are no different. They swim in so much data that they rarely know what to do with it, much less how to compare multiple data sets to understand and explore the true stories behind the data.

## STRENGTHS-BASED DECISION-MAKING

Teams activate an asset-centered mindset while engaging in data-driven decision-making. It will amplify students' strengths and assets before discussing their next level of development. Using an asset-centered approach reinforces what is working, such as content students have mastered or skills and dispositions that they can build upon (Bocala and Boudett, 2022). Disrupting deficit-oriented practices is difficult. They are systemic and culturally ingrained. Just watch the evening news or attend a school board meeting across many parts of our country. Our culture is often fueled by otherizing, blaming, shaming, hating, and fearing the "'other." When teachers engage in deficit thinking about their students, it results in negative beliefs about them and their communities (Nelson and Guerra, 2014). This mindset limits teacher expectations about student accomplishments. The Visible Learning research backs this up. A teacher's estimate of achievement is based on past experiences (Hattie, 2023). When teachers positively estimate student achievements, it shifts perceptions about students and decisions about what approaches to take. The weighted mean effect size for this influence is 1.29. That translates into having the potential to considerably accelerate student learning (Hattie, 2023). When teachers make positive estimates, students learn more.

## THE INVESTIGATIVE PROCESS

After teams design their "blueprint for inquiry," they begin an investigative process. They use multiple evidence sources to assess their prototype and determine its impact on students. Teams collectively act, making midcourse corrections based on data monitoring progress. Quantitative and qualitative evidence gives insight into the impact on student learning. The inquiry process is iterative, and it can feel messy to some educators, making them feel uncomfortable. Quality peer facilitation supports teams and ensures focused team meetings that support knowledge sharing, reflection, and knowledge building. This process requires critical thinking and reasoning. Teams continually adapt their inquiry based on findings. Sometimes teams refine their inquiry, and sometimes they cannot answer questions. Teams deepen their knowledge by working with experts in the field, tapping into expertise within their system, and using professional literature. The knowledge gained from inquiry contributes to the collective knowledge of the system. When PLCs, MTSS, or SEL teams engage in this process, they make decisions in partnership with their students and families. They offer the kinds of support learners need. In a collaborative inquiry cycle, educators

- commit to a common goal and focus
- develop a plan using the Impact Team Blueprint
- implement the plan by collecting and analyzing evidence
- determine its impact
- refine actions based on current data
- reflect with each other and students

Figure 7.1 illustrates this iterative inquiry process. Teams use inquiry to monitor progress and to determine the levels of support (MTSS) students need during PLC time.

**Figure 7.1: The Impact Teams Multi-Tiered Systems of Support (MTSS) Model**

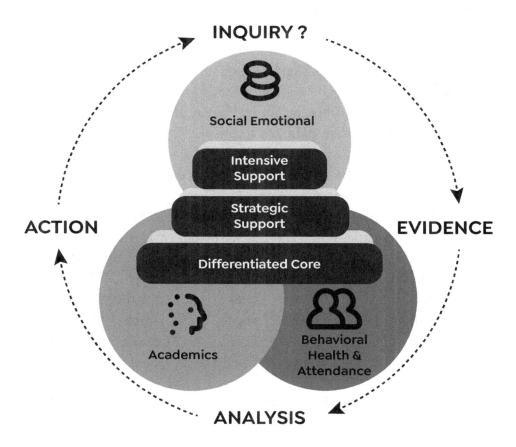

Adapted from: https://www.branchingminds.com/mtss-guide

## Personal Reflection

☐ How do you ensure that all students needs are met?

# WHAT MAKES QUALITY EVIDENCE

Learning organizations recognize the importance of holistic and robust evidence. It informs continuous improvement cycles across all Impact Teams (PLCs, ILTs, district ILTs, SEL, equity, school boards, etc.). Teams employ various strategies to collect and analyze data (Evidence–Analysis– Action [EAA]) to make informed decisions about instructional practices and policies. Schools use qualitative and quantitative data to drive continuous improvement efforts and Impact Team inquiry.

The Impact Team model has evolved since 2017. Teams nationally use qualitative data more and more to make better, responsive partnership decisions. Triangulating qualitative evidence with quantitative data gives teachers a more robust story about the learners behind the data. It offers insight into attitudes, beliefs, and experiences that quantitative data can't convey. Safir and Dugan (2021) discuss the concept of "street data" when engaging in data-driven decision making. The authors define street data as "the qualitative and experiential data that emerges at eye level and on lower frequencies when we train our brains to discern it" (p.2). Street data is qualitative and experiential asset-based evidence. It is the lived experiences of stakeholders we note through observations, active listening, and student learning artifacts. When teams collect and analyze *street data*, they learn to see what is right with students rather than focusing on their deficits (Safir & Dugan, 2021). Impact Teams use asset-based inquiry to look for bright spots. They use multiple evidence sources to clarify assets and define next learning steps.

**Tip 7.1: Model of Success:** Learn how K-8 Impact Teams used SEL evidence to cultivate healthy learning identities in their students from former Harlem K-8 principal Jeneca Parker.

Here are some common categories of evidence.
- **Quantitative Data:** This includes numerical data collected through surveys, criterion-based formative and summative assessments (student work), criterion-based performance assessment, standardized tests, universal screeners, diagnostic assessments, and other quantitative measures. It provides objective information that can be analyzed statistically to identify patterns, trends, and correlations.
- **Qualitative Data:** Qualitative data encompasses non-numerical information obtained through observations, interviews, focus groups, and open-ended responses. It offers deeper insights into attitudes, beliefs, and experiences, providing a rich understanding of the context and nuances of particular issues.
- **Research Studies:** Organizations often rely on research studies conducted by experts in the field. These academic journal studies provide evidence-based insights into effective practices, interventions, and proven strategies that yield positive results.
- **Best Practices:** Organizations look for best practices (that have demonstrated success in achieving desired outcomes) within their industry or in related fields. They provide guidance and serve as benchmarks for continuous improvement.
- **Case Studies:** Case studies involve in-depth analyses of specific situations, programs, or initiatives. They provide detailed accounts of successes, challenges, and lessons learned. They offer valuable insights and practical examples to inform decision-making and improvement efforts.
- **Collaborative Inquiry:** Collaborative inquiry or action research involves conducting research within an organization to address specific practice puzzles. Organizations collect data, analyze it, and make informed decisions (EAA) based on their context and unique needs.

## Perception Data

Perception data (voice data) refers to information derived from subjective perceptions, opinions, and beliefs rather than objective or quantifiable measurements. We collect perception data through surveys, interviews, focus groups, and other qualitative research methods. Perception data can be qualitative or quantitative depending on the method. This kind of data is valuable for understanding how individuals perceive and interpret various aspects of an organization, program, or initiative. It potentially provides insights into an individual's attitudes, feelings, and beliefs, offering a glimpse into lived experiences and perspectives. This type of data sheds light on satisfaction, engagement, motivation, perceptions of fairness, and overall experiences.

Researchers often use perception data in combination with other types of evidence to gain a comprehensive situational understanding or to inform the data-driven decision-making processes. By incorporating perception data, organizations gain a deeper understanding of stakeholders' viewpoints and preferences, which helps shape strategies, policies, and interventions to better meet needs.

When organizations make decisions about policies and practices, including the voices of stakeholders is essential. Making informed decisions that include the voice of stakeholders ensures that organizations gain a comprehensive understanding of their strengths, obstacles, and areas for improvement; this inclusive practice drives asset-based continuous improvement.

# THE ROLE OF EVIDENCE IN PROFESSIONAL TEAMING TO LEARN

Impact Teams serve a purpose; they relentlessly advance learner agency through continuous improvement cycles. They anchor their inquiry using multiple evidence sources. They collectively act based on that evidence. Impact Teams can engage in inquiry at all levels of a system. The evidence teams analyze is dependent on their purpose.

The following examples illustrate the alignment of multiple evidence sources, which teams use to make inclusive decisions. Read the examples below to see how different teams use evidence to inform and act. The examples are simplified to ensure clarity.

### Example 1: District-Level Impact Teams

**Who:** Board members, members of the cabinet, community partners, family partners, curriculum and instruction teams, school safety teams, and more can compose a district-level Impact Team.

**Possible Puzzles of Practice:** District Impact Teams may focus inquiry on many practice puzzles connected to district goals: (1) diversity, belonging, equity, and inclusion; (2) curricular; (3) instructional leadership; (4) data use; (5) equitable parent engagement, and more.

**Example Inquiry Questions:** To what degree have we implemented our assessment for a learning (A4L) initiative over the past 3 years? How can we strengthen implementation of A4L? What are our strengths? What are our greatest opportunities? Who needs the most support? How can we be sure that our most misrepresented students engage deeply? Who hasn't been impacted by the power of A4L practices? Why?

**If** a district's goal is to implement assessment for learning (A4L) in K-12 classrooms,

**Then** the district team may collect and analyze the following sources of evidence to ensure quality implementation of assessment for learning:
• organizational network mapping about the informal social network
• teacher and principal perception (survey) data about their confidence in implementation of A4L
  ◻ teacher–principal focus groups or 1:1 interviews to illuminate baseline evidence statements from the survey
• student perception (survey) data about their confidence using A4L practices

▫ student and family focus groups or 1:1 interviews to illuminate baseline evidence statements from the survey
- family perception (survey) data regarding A4L practices knowledge levels and how these practices impact their children
  ▫ student–family focus groups or 1:1 interviews to illuminate baseline evidence statements from the survey
- Observation data via Danielson 3-D and/or instructional rounds

### Example 2: School-Based Equity Teams

**Who:** Parent-caregiver and student representation from historically misrepresented communities, families, and student representatives from all demographic groups, ILT members, counselors, social workers, administration, and others can compose an Impact Team.

**Possible Puzzles of Practice:** School-based equity teams may focus their inquiry on: (1) evaluating school policies that may cause learning barriers, (2) student performance gaps caused by systemic opportunity gaps, and (3) contributions to the school-to-prison pipeline.

**Example Inquiry Questions:** To what degree does a student's sense of belonging impact their learning life at our school? What are our strengths? Who is in greatest need? What systemic barriers may present obstacles for students? Who *wasn't* impacted by a low sense of belonging? Why?

**If** a school equity team wants to understand their students' sense of belonging,

**Then** the school equity team may collect and analyze the following sources of evidence to ensure quality implementation of school climate goals (belonging):
- student and family perception survey data regarding belonging and relational trust

**Example 2, continued**

- ￭ student–family focus groups, 1:1 interviews, or reflections to illuminate baseline survey results
- · suspension, referral, and attendance data
  - ￭ student–family focus groups, 1:1 interviews, and/or student–family reflections to illuminate baseline evidence statements from suspension, referral, and attendance data
- · graduation rates or pass/fail rates
  - ￭ student–family focus groups, 1:1 interviews, or reflections to illuminate baseline evidence statements about graduation rates or pass/fail rates
- · freshman pass/fail rates, followed up by qualitative methods 1-1 interviews or focus groups
- · universal screening data from the students most impacted by the problem, followed up by qualitative methods

**Example 3: Instructional Leadership Teams**

**Who:** Student representation that reflects student demographic groups, school leadership, grade-level or department leads, a counselor, a social worker, a special education representation or others can compose an instructional leadership Impact Team.

**Possible Puzzles of Practice:** For example, ILTs may focus on: (1) school policies that may cause learning barriers and harm, (2) student performance gaps caused by systemic opportunity gaps, 3) longstanding opportunity gaps, (4) issues related to curriculum and instruction, or (5) determining and supporting equity goals.

**Example Inquiry Questions:** To what degree do our school systems contribute to the school-to-prison pipeline? Who has the greatest need? Why? Who does not have the greatest need? Why? What existing practices may harm students and families? Why?

**If** an ILT was interested in the degree that school policies, systems, and practices contribute to the school-to-prison pipeline,

**Then** the ILT may collect and analyze the following evidence to define puzzles of practice related to the school-to-prison pipeline:
- student and family perception survey data regarding sense of belonging and relational trust
  - student–family focus groups or 1:1 interviews or reflections to illuminate baseline evidence survey statements
- educator perception (survey) data regarding policies and practices that may harm students
  - focus group or 1:1 interviews regarding policies and practices that may harm students
- suspension, referral, and attendance data
  - student–family focus groups, 1:1 interviews, or reflections to illuminate baseline evidence survey statements
- graduation rates or pass/fail rates
  - student–family focus groups, 1:1 interviews, or reflections to illuminate baseline evidence statements about graduation rates or pass/fail rates
- freshman pass/fail rates, followed up by qualitative methods
  - universal screening data from the students most impacted by the problem, followed up by qualitative methods

### Example 4: English Learner Advisory Councils (ELAC)

**Who:** In California, schools must have an English Learner Advisory Council (ELAC) if they have 21 or more multilingual learners. Families and caregivers, school staff who support multilingual learners, and community members typically make up this Impact Team.

**Possible Puzzles of Practice:** An ELAC may focus their inquiry on (1) advising school officials regarding multilingual learner programs and services, (2) adequate yearly progress in language acquisition compared with performance

**Example 4, continued**

on universal screeners and state tests, or (3) multilingual learners' overall sense of belonging.

**Inquiry Questions:** To what degree does our ELL program ensure students make annual language acquisition goals? Who has the greatest need? Why? Who does not have the greatest need? Why? What existing practices may harm students and families? Why?

**If** an ELAC engages in this inquiry to determine the impact of their ELL program and/or to realize goals related to multilingual learner achievement,

**Then** the ELAC may collect and analyze the following sources of evidence to define puzzles of practice related to the quality of their ELL program:
· Annual English language proficiency assessment results
· Formative language assessment data
· Universal screening data disaggregated by demographic groups
· Frequency of student talk during systematic English language development
· Survey students and parents about the quality of support they receive.

**Example 5: Early Literacy PLCs**

**Who:** A kindergarten, first- or second-grade team, interventionist, instructional coach, school leadership, special education teacher, ELL support teacher or others may comprise an early literacy Impact Team.

**Possible Puzzles of Practice:** Puzzles of practice regarding progress and mastery of: (1) reading foundation skills dedicated to phonemic awareness, phonics, and sight words, (2) writing progress, (3) oral language development, (4) comprehension and ability to retell and recount, (5) math fluency and problem-solving, (6) social awareness, or (7) SEL goals.

**Inquiry Question(s):** What is the impact of our systematic instruction in

Example 5, continued

phonemic awareness, phonics and sight words? What are our students' greatest strengths? What are their greatest opportunities? Who has been harmed the most by the lack of mastery? Why? Who has not been harmed? Why? How does the lack of mastery reveal itself in social and emotional well-being? How will this impact their lives?

**If** a first-grade PLC engages in an inquiry regarding the mastery of reading foundation skills on students' reading identity,

**Then** the first-grade team may collect and analyze the following evidence to define puzzles of practice and/or to realize their early literacy reading goals:
• universal screening data (like Acadience Learning, i-Ready, or MAP)
• educator perception (survey) data regarding confidence in research-based methods
• comprehension diagnostics and running records
• reading identity interviews
• writing samples
• SEL data (like the DESSA evidence-based SEL inventory)
• observation
• 1:1 parent-caregiver conferences
• student conferences

The latter examples illustrate how Impact Teams analyze multiple sources of data (data triangulation) to make informed decisions about student or organizational needs. Typically teams use 3-4 sources of evidence (quantitative and qualitative) when engaged in collaborative inquiry. Keep in mind that a team's inquiry question and theory of action determine the evidence base.

## Personal Reflection

☐ What did you learn from reading through the various samples?

☐ What did they have in common?

☐ How are the examples similar to or different from what your teams do?

☐ What did you notice about the relationship between quantitative and qualitative data collection?

# EVIDENCE OF LEARNER AGENCY

Impact Teams (PLCs) scale up pedagogies that advance learner agency, including core formative practices (self-assessment, peer assessment, accountable talk, reflection, inclusive questioning, and feedback) that emphasize self-regulation and metacognition. These practices transfer to college, career, and life. Teams use quality evidence to monitor their theory of action. We developed these examples to provide clarity.

**Example 1: Inquiry Focused on Student Reflection**

· **If** a team scales up student reflection because they want to increase students' self-awareness concerning academic progress,

· **Then** the team may collect and analyze the following evidence:

 ▫ CFAs (criteria-based common formative assessments),

 ▫ CFA student reflections

 ▫ DESSA SEL screener data aligned to self-awareness and goal-directed behavior

 ▫ Universal screener data to benchmark performance expectations.

· **Then** they would take collective action based on their analysis.

**Example 2: Inquiry Focused on Student Goal Setting**

· **If** a team focused on student goal-directed behavior and self-awareness,

· **Then** the team may collect and analyze the following evidence:

 ▫ Student goals

 ▫ Universal screener data

 ▫ Student work or CFAs (criterion-based common formative assessments)

 ▫ Portfolio evidence reflecting student goals

**Example 2, continued**

  ▫ Observation of accountable talk in relationship to goal setting
  ▫ 1:1 meetings or focus groups
· **Then** they would take collective action based on their analysis.

**Example 3: Inquiry Focused on Peer Assessment and Accountable Talk**

· **If** a team focused on student peer assessment integrated with accountable talk,
· **Then** the team may collect and analyze the following evidence:
  ▫ Peer and self-assessment observations
  ▫ Student reflections on their confidence when engaging in peer and self-assessment
  ▫ Student work and/or CFAs (criterion-based common formative assessment)
  ▫ Universal screening data
  ▫ Student voice through interviews or focus groups
· **Then,** the team would take collective action based on their analysis.

Each example clearly influences the advance learner agency and the evidence a team would collect and analyze to know if their inquiry positively impacted students.

## Team Reflection

☐ What did you notice about the examples? How are these examples similar or different to your current practices?

☐ Why did teams consider more than one source of evidence?

☐ What evidence does your PLC use?

☐ How is your PLC developing learners' agency? What is your evidence?

# THE *WHY:* RESEARCH AND REASONS

High-quality evidence provides the team with current insights into the learning process. It prompts reflection, stimulates dialogue and debate, and fosters critical thinking around what, why, and how students learn.

## REASON 1: FOCUSING ON ASSETS COUNTERACTS DEFICIT-ORIENTED PRACTICES.

Using data to highlight students' strengths and assets before describing their next level of development counteracts deficit-oriented practices. It reinforces what works, such as content students have mastered or skills they can build upon (Bocala & Boudett, 2022).

## REASON 2: EQUITABLE DATA USE HONORS STUDENTS' FUNDS OF KNOWLEDGE.

Asset-centered approaches highlight goodness, strength, and resilience when engaging in data-driven decision-making (Lawrence-Lightfoot & Davis, 1997). It recognizes that students have "funds of knowledge" from lived experiences, families, friends, and cultural backgrounds (González et al., 2005).

## REASON 3: QUALITY CURRICULUM IMPROVES THE QUALITY OF TEACHING.

Students must have access to the curriculum to learn (see Chapter 5). And for them to access the curriculum, teachers need to understand students' positions within learning progressions. So teachers need to gather *evidence* to understand what students know and can do. With that *evidence*, teachers can design lessons for all students. A key "signpost" of excellence in education is when teachers engage in *"critical reflection in light of evidence about their teaching"* (Hattie 2009).

## REASON 4: QUALITY CURRICULUM IMPROVES STUDENT LEARNING.

We all learn by linking new ideas to what we already know. We gather *evidence* through feedback from the teacher, peers, and ourselves to discover what we know. Note that discovery is not just for the teacher—most importantly, it's for the student. For example, creating a learning portfolio based on success criteria and/or key competencies *evidences* progress and indicates learning strengths. Receiving teacher and peer feedback based on success criteria is *evidence* that leads to analysis. That, in turn, accelerates learning (Black & Wiliam, 1998).

## REASON 5: WELL-PLANNED ASSESSMENT IS A SPRINGBOARD FOR ACTION.

Analyzing quality evidence is important professional dialogue, but it is only an intellectual exercise unless followed by action. Base the action on specific quality evidence to ensure appropriate instructional responses. If the evidence is not current (old) or too general (not specific to a learning goal or rubric), then instructional decisions will rarely succeed. Are you making instructional decisions based on last year's test scores? Evidence is like feedback—it needs to be timely, relevant, and specific!

# THE *HOW:* FOUR PURPOSEFUL PROTOCOLS

All 10 purposeful protocols use quality evidence to inform decisions. In this chapter, we emphasize four protocols that use evidence to enhance collaborative inquiry.

1. Analysis of Evidence (AOE)

2. Calibration

3. Check-In

4. Case Study

# ANALYSIS OF EVIDENCE (AOE) UNPACKED

Impact Teams (or PLCs use) quality evidence as the critical foundation for data-driven decision-making. PLCs always analyze student work (products and performances) to monitor the theory of action progress. They ensure formative and summative tasks are criterion-based to clarify assessment criteria. Teams always co-construct criteria with students to create crystal clear expectations. Criterion-based common formative assessment measures a learner's academic performance against standards-based competencies or success criteria. The success criteria provide progress markers. They triangulate data from at least two other sources (qualitative and quantitative) to ensure a holistic student performance view. PLCs typically use student voice data to clearly perceive how students view themselves as learners. Many teams use universal screening data or observation data as well.

Quality student learning evidence can take on multiple forms, including

- universal screener data or diagnostic measures
- criterion-based student work samples
- criterion-based e-portfolios
- peer and self-assessment and reflections
- observation notes or videos
- nonverbal communication observations
- SEL data (DESSA, Panorama)
- student voice data (focus groups, 1:1 conferences, surveys, etc.)
- a range of products or performances aligned to success criteria

Quality evidence provides feedback to the team and learner, providing the basis for focused dialogue. The evidence must be:

- specific to learning
- agreed upon in advance
- visible
- authentic
- used to focus conversations
- the foundation of the analysis
- a springboard to action.

Without quality evidence, teaming is just another personal opinions forum. With quality evidence, the dialogue leads to analysis—and analysis leads to collective action.

Based on the analysis of evidence, teams determine root causes. They anchor collective actions in evidence-based practices with the potential to accelerate learning. Teams typically use strategies that emphasize self-regulation and metacognition since these influences get some of the highest effects and support students with metacognition (See Chapter 1). Learning to learn strategies are not only useful in school; they are useful in life.

# EXAMPLE OF AOE PROTOCOL: EAA ANALYSIS OF STUDENT WORK

Analyzing student work gives educators information and feedback about a student's understanding of their knowledge, skills, dispositions, and strategies. When coupled with students' reflections, self-assessment, or peer assessments, Impact Teams gain a more holistic view of how students perceive themselves as learners.

## Launching the Meeting with Student Assets at the Center

Teams often begin their analysis by opening dialogue about their students' assets, especially those who still need to build mastery of prerequisite knowledge, skills, and dispositions. We often marginalize these students in team meetings with a laser-like focus on their deficits. These deficit-minded practices must change; they harm students. We are not saying that it isn't good practice to target the knowledge, skills, and dispositions students must develop, but we can get there through asset-based dialogues that lift our students up. Identifying the learning the student "has in their toolkit" allows us to build upon that knowledge. Many students need some light coaching to connect to their strengths outside of the classroom or in other courses. For example, my (Paul) son Alex struggled in math. He would freeze up, hated math, and developed low self-efficacy. From my perspective, he was an advanced problem solver. His father and I experienced his mad "problem-solving ability" daily. He could have drawn upon many examples if his teachers had viewed his life experiences as valuable "knowledge" to build upon. If there was a genuine interest in the funds of knowledge Alex brought to class, his teachers would have perceived him as an expert learner as he walked through the door. Alex's experience was different. The school community perceived him as a failure, and he agreed with them. He took Algebra three times, and math became a gatekeeper for him. Alex just needed to know that he *already was a problem solver.*

Here is an example of this practice in action. This sixth-grade ELA team analyzes summaries to determine next steps.

Facilitator: *I am so grateful we have this time together today. Our goal for today is to analyze student work to determine what students need next. We are looking at this work formatively today so we get the feedback we need to scale up and refine our feedback practices in class. As always, let's reconnect with our agreements. I would like you to pick one agreement that resonates with you today and explain why. Remember, our agreements are aspirational and reflect who we strive to be.*

*>> The Impact Team takes 3 to 5 minutes to share. Example agreements are in Chapter 3.*

Facilitator: *Today, we will launch by spending 5 to 10 minutes engaging in dialogue around our learning that needs the most support. Let's start our inquiry by analyzing some work samples from a particular group of students. Our goal is to brainstorm the assets in their work and learning habits. You can also take some time to analyze their accompanying reflections since the perception data will give you insight into how they were feeling when engaging in the task. Reflections give us a window into their thinking and a sense of their personal goals. You can also draw on your knowledge of their learning habits. Many students reflect on their habits, so we will also speak to them.*

*>> The team takes a couple of minutes to gather their ideas.*

Facilitator: *Okay, let's share what we have learned about these particular learners. Even though they may have struggled with the task's success criteria, we can help them build on many things. Let's take some time to figure them out. Many things we discuss will apply to what that student needs in other performance bands.*

| EVIDENCE | ANALYSIS | ACTION |
|---|---|---|
| What are their social, emotional, and academic assets? | What knowledge, skills, and dispositions led to this success? Why were they successful? | What's next for these learners? |
| • They really stuck with the task this time<br>• Based on many of their reflections, we can see that they thought about their learning habits.<br>  □ Many referred to having to be patient with themselves when they got stuck.<br>  □ Some mentioned activating their problem-solving superpower. | • All the disposition work we have been doing is paying off. They are speaking about the "learning to learn" habits we have unpacked in class.<br>• They connected personal experiences to the habits of learning needed to be successful with this task<br>• They knew discussing things helped them learn more. | • Sustain the "habit of learning work" and the "learning to learn" strategy work. It is paying off.<br>• Maybe have the ones who created a graphic organizer share that strategy with other students who could benefit from it.<br>• What if the learners who annotated share their strategy too? I have a lot of kids in other performance bands that need that tip too. |

| EVIDENCE | ANALYSIS | ACTION |
|---|---|---|
| ▫ Some students mentioned needing more time to "talk it out." <br>• Many could speak to the overall topic and knew what the article was about. <br>• They used text features to figure out key points. (You can see it in their annotations.) <br>• Some students summarized a TED Talk they were interested in. Many drew the graphic organizer we discussed in class to organize their thinking. | • They used a simple graphic organizer that they could draw. <br>• They knew it was okay to be stuck. (They used our "I'm stuck" strategy and wrote about it in their reflection.) <br>• They knew that authors use features to get their key points across. <br>• They used the title and features to name the overall topic. <br>• They knew that annotation helps them make meaning. <br>• The students who chose to summarize a podcast or TED Talk knew that the success criteria for a summary transferred to other mediums. | • Let's start nudging some to apply their knowledge to summarizing a text. They can continue to choose a few articles that interest them. <br>• What if we had them do this for a purpose? What if they taught others about a topic they love? That would pull learners in. <br><br>***Visible Learning influences reflected in team actions.*** <br>• *Reciprocal teaching* <br>• *Highlighting and underlining* <br>• *Self-assessment* <br>• *Summarizing* <br>• *Classroom discussion* <br>• *Feedback* <br>• *Small group instruction* |

Facilitator: *Great, now we have a plan. Our learners can assist with all the resources they need. They can find them since we use texts, podcasts, and videos that interest them. Once we build capacity with them, they can try summarizing in their other courses. We can let the full school know what we are doing in our schoolwide Google Chat. I know other teachers who can pitch in and help.*

## Personal Reflection

The team in this example started their analysis by discussing the students who needed the most support. This example reflects high-impact methods with the potential to accelerate learning. The team started this by charting their assets.

- ☐ What did you value about this example?

- ☐ How is this practice similar to or different from what you already do?

- ☐ What do you notice about the "spirit" of the conversation?

- ☐ What did the peer facilitator do? Was it effective?

- ☐ Did this conversation move learning forward? Why or why not?

Let's discuss this protocol in the context of the team's inquiry. It scaled self-assessment because students determined unactionable goals due to a lack of information. We simplified this example for clarity. It highlights the "approaching proficiency" performance band. These students needed to build expertise in 1 or 2 criteria to show mastery. Typically, teams analyze at least three performance levels, use the evidence to refine Tier 1 differentiation and determine other tiered support if needed. This process allows teams to "progress monitor" between universal screening. We kept the notes from this meeting so teams can use evidence to make decisions with students about support tiers. The more students engage in the decision-making process, the more they will gain critical decision-making expertise. This ensures that we are not "doing school to kids." We engage them as learning partners.

| EVIDENCE | ANALYSIS | ACTION |
|---|---|---|
| **Close to Proficiency** | | |
| > What did they do well? | > What led to their success? | > What's next for these learners? |
| **· The main idea clearly stated** | · Ability to determine the importance and recognize connections and patterns across the text | · *Paraphrasing* |
| **· At least 3 key details that support the main idea** | | > What approaches will we use? |
| **· Details come from each text section** | · Many students activated learning habits and referred to them in reflections | · *Co-construct success criteria with examples of quality paraphrasing* |
| · Details are paraphrased | · Many annotated the text for the criteria | · *Students will self-assess using the success criteria (.75 ES)* |
| **· Used expert words from the text** | · Some used the "context clue" strategy | · *Students revise their work based on self-assessment* |
| **· The short conclusion that connects back to the main idea** | · Many students circled the repeated words | |
| | · They knew the structure of a summary | > What organizational strategy will you use? |
| *Universal Design for Learning (UDL) Notes:* | · They all chose articles that interested them | · *Small group instruction 2 times a week for 3 weeks* |
| · *Students can choose to summarize articles, videos, or podcasts to ensure accessibility.* | · Some chose TED Talks, and they used Cornell Notes to track thinking | > What resources will you need? |
| · *Speechify to read aloud PDFs* | | · *Nonfiction articles* |
| · *Sentence stems and frames* | | · *Exemplars of paraphrasing* |
| · *Exemplars* | | · *Success criteria for paraphrasing* |
| · *Graphic organizers that they choose* | | |

| EVIDENCE | ANALYSIS | ACTION |
|---|---|---|
| **Close to Proficiency** | | |
| What criteria do they need the most support with? <br> • *Many struggled to paraphrase key details* | Why do you think that? <br> • They may need help understanding the concept of paraphrasing and why they need it in their life. <br> • *Maybe they have never done it.* <br> • *They may need more models.* <br><br> How can we build from their assets? <br> • *Invite them to make connections to their own life. Many do it orally and don't even know they are paraphrasing.* <br> • *They paraphrase all the time on social media.* | ***Visible Learning influences reflected in team actions.*** <br> • *Reciprocal teaching* <br> • *Success criteria* <br> • *Self-assessment* <br> • *Summarizing* <br> • *Classroom discussion* <br> • *Feedback* <br> • *Small group instruction* |
| *The process continues with other performance bands.* | | |

## Reading Between the Lines

Sometimes the data tells a story but we have to dig deeper to find the true root cause(s). As teams collect and analyze student evidence from other performance bands, they begin by discussing their learners' strengths, what led to their strengths, and how they can sustain and develop existing strengths. When teams engage in "knowledge/skill gap analysis" they analyze the evidence to determine the probable root cause(s) based on the evidence. Teams typically need to triangulate data based on the gaps they have identified. For example, they may see that many students had difficulties identifying text structure. However, teams need to dig deeper and read between the lines. They need to ask themselves if text structure is really the obstacle. This kind of curiosity drives more action. The team may dig into their diagnostic reading data to see if these students have mastery of reading foundation skills. If the students don't have mastery of reading foundation skills the team may be closer to identifying the true "root cause". If teams are truly curious, they keep searching. They may find that many of the students in the group they are investigating may have moved from school to school, this mobility has a negative impact on student learning. If the team's curiosity persists, they may dig deeper to determine root cause(s). If the school is trauma aware, they may look to other sources of evidence to see if trauma may be impacting a student's learning. Having an "inquiry mindset" is critical to understanding impact.

The "peer facilitator" uses specific facilitation moves to support their team in developing an "inquiry mindset" during data analysis. Teams slowly but surely embody an "inquiry mindset" with deliberate practice. They constantly question the evidence until they determine the root cause(s). Parent advice is also an effective source of evidence when determining root cause(s). As students get older, teams can get advice from them directly. This kind of curiosity propels teams to offer the right kind of tiered support that matches their needs. The example peer facilitation questions below illustrate the power of quality peer facilitation questions that drive quality data analysis.

## Gap Analysis Example Facilitation Questions:

- Why is the student(s) struggling with _____? What evidence do you have that supports your analysis?
- Do we have other evidence that may illuminate our understanding of this obstacle for students?
- What prerequisite knowledge and/or skills do they need to be successful? Do we have any evidence that helps us understand their mastery of prerequisite skills? What is the evidence and what can we learn from it?

- Is trauma a factor? Why or why not? What evidence do we have that suggests that trauma is a factor?
- Is the curriculum a factor? Why do we think that?
- Are learning habits a factor? Why do we think that?
- Are there any early warning signals in the data that may help us understand their needs better? What are they?
- Are there obstacles within our control that students have to overcome? What are they? What can we do to disrupt them?

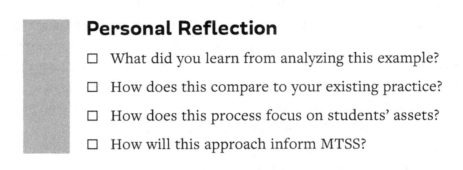

## Personal Reflection

☐ What did you learn from analyzing this example?

☐ How does this compare to your existing practice?

☐ How does this process focus on students' assets?

☐ How will this approach inform MTSS?

# CALIBRATION UNPACKED

This protocol ensures accurately, consistently scored student work, known as inter-rater reliability. Teachers use student work samples to calibrate and anchor their understanding about student progress. (See the Unpacking for Clarity Protocol for related information on formative assessment.)

## Calibration Protocol Example

In this example, teams calibrated their understanding of proficiency to ensure inter-rater reliability. They brought proficient summary examples to the team meeting. They used success criteria to build consensus about proficiency. They refined the criteria based on their analysis. They left the meeting with 10 to 15 examples of high-quality work to share with students.

| EVIDENCE | ANALYSIS | ACTION |
|---|---|---|
| **Close to Proficiency** | | |
| Samples from each classroom represent teachers' understanding of proficiency.<br><br>**Task Success Criteria:**<br>• *The main idea clearly stated*<br>• *At least 3 key details support the main idea*<br>• *Details come from each text section*<br>• *The student paraphrased details*<br>• *Expert words appeared*<br>• *A short conclusion connected back to the main idea* | **What is our consensus on the matter of proficiency?**<br>• *Strong alignment regarding stating the main idea and paraphrasing details*<br><br>**Where do we disagree?**<br>• *Our scores regarding gathering details and use of vocabulary/ expert words vary.*<br>• *Some of the team members did not note the lack of a conclusion because they had not taught it yet, skewing the results.* | **How can we ensure greater inter-rater reliability?**<br>• *Clarify expectations about gathering details from throughout the text and the use of expert words*<br>• *Teach students to write conclusions and provide opportunities for practice and feedback*<br>• *Co-construct an annotated writing progression based on various samples*<br>• *Update the rubric and other tools*<br><br>**Which organizational strategy will you use?**<br>• *Re-engage students in whole and small-group instruction to deepen their understanding of the updated criteria*<br><br>What resources will you need?<br>• *State standards resources*<br>• *Newly annotated examples*<br>• *A co-constructed writing progression* |

# CHECK-IN PROTOCOL UNPACKED

Tracking teaching impact via student progress is a noble goal, but it must be realistic. This protocol helps teams monitor the effectiveness of collective actions and agreements. The team frequently shares successes and challenges, then course corrections as needed. They can use Google Meet to collaborate virtually or check in asynchronously using Google Chat. Both approaches save time.

## Check-In EAA Protocol Example

Based on the AOE example, the Impact Team 'checked in' on the impact of their evidence-based strategies for each performance band. In this example, they use the strategies as evidence. They systematically monitor student groups to see if their selected strategies are impactful. If so, they sustain that practice. If not, they midcourse correct.

| EVIDENCE | ANALYSIS | ACTION | |
|---|---|---|---|
| **Performance Band: Close to Proficiency** | | | |
| What were the strategies we selected when analyzing work last week? <br>• *Co-construct success criteria with examples of quality paraphrasing* <br>• *Students self-assess using the success criteria (.75 ES)* <br>• *Students revise summaries based on self-assessment and teacher feedback* | Are our strategies impactful? Why? Why not? <br>• *The examples we used from calibration ensure clarity* <br>• *Students compared their work to the samples we provided using co-construction. They identify the criteria in their work because they developed them.* <br>• *They coded their work by the success criteria, but self-assessment needs more consistency.* | ***Revisions were okay but not proficient.*** **To improve self-assessment, we will:** <br>• Offer more revision models that use feedback, success criteria, and student work samples <br>• Students will revise a common example with a partner <br>• Provide revision feedback to each partnership <br>• Students will choose to work solo, with a partner, or with a teacher | |

| EVIDENCE | ANALYSIS | ACTION |
|---|---|---|
|  | • *They may need more models.*<br>• **Revisions were okay but not proficient because the revised products did not match the quality of the exemplars** |  |

Teacher teams 'check in' on each student's performance band. Remember: the least experienced students will receive the same approaches but will use UDL to ensure access.

## Personal Reflection

☐ How do your teams engage in dialogue about strategic impacts? Why? How does this example compare to your current practice?

☐ How does this protocol ensure quality implementation?

☐ What are your next steps?

# CASE STUDY PROTOCOL UNPACKED

Teams use the Case Study Protocol to study students who need extra support. Long-standing systemic barriers outside the student's or teachers' control generally impact these students. Teachers can only use strategies within their locus of control. When teams use the 'Case Study Protocol' they put emphasis on identifying their learners' funds of knowledge to build differentiated and personalized learning plans. They remove systemic barriers as much as possible. Teams gather evidence from parents about their child's learning passions and about how their child learns best. Teams analyze all evidence to create supportive actions for these students. They can serve these students using Tier 2 and Tier 3 support. Systemic obstacles sometimes require policy revisions to avoid harm.

## Case Study Protocol Example

Based on the AOE example from this section, the Impact Team aimed to identify which students needed help attaining the goals. Several students were newcomers to the country and learning multiple languages. Teachers teamed to collect and study related evidence. The school social worker, counselor, and ESL teachers joined this meeting.

*Sources of Evidence:* Observation, ACEs results, ELL screener data, reading foundation screener.

| EVIDENCE | ANALYSIS | ACTION |
|---|---|---|
| What are these student assets? | What led to their strengths? | What are our next steps? |
| • *They want to learn. They try a lot.*<br>• *They love nonfiction the most—especially animal books.*<br>• *They can point at pictures and say simple words.*<br>• *They share pictures of their family.*<br>• *When we model, they try to follow along.*<br>• *They learn initial sounds and survival words like drink, bathroom, etc.*<br>• *They have lots of friends*<br>• *They speak fluent Russian (I need clarification on other languages).* | • *They developed perseverance before coming to us.*<br>• *They must have been good readers and writers in their home language ( we had a para who spoke Russian work with them).*<br>• *They love using Google Translate.*<br>• *Three of them can draw beautifully; they must have loved to draw and had a lot of practice.*<br>• *They learned a lot of sounds—maybe they transferred those sounds from L1.* | • *Get more counseling support from someone who can support them in their L1.*<br>• *Possible health screening.*<br>• *Small group work on foundational reading skills at their point of need.*<br>• *Computer-adaptive support on Lexia learning.*<br>• *Targeted designated instruction at their language level for 45–60 minutes daily.*<br>• *Audio and video books.*<br>• *Imagine Learning for 20 minutes daily.* |

| EVIDENCE | ANALYSIS | ACTION |
|---|---|---|
| Greatest growth opportunities: <br> • *They need to learn all of their letters and sight words.* <br> • *They easily become frustrated.* <br> • *Loud noises scare them.* <br> • *Sometimes they struggle to focus.* | What is the story behind the evidence? <br> • *We worry about the impact of war trauma.* <br> • *They struggle with emotional regulation; they may not feel safe.* <br> • *They may need more peer-peer support.* <br> • *Language and trauma likely impact them.* | • *Hone our Google Translate skills.* <br> • *Create an affinity group so they can partner with older kids from Russia.* <br> • *Get a translator.* <br> • *Ask parents-caregivers for using cultural synchronization questions from the National Equity Project to learn about their funds of knowledge.* <br> • *Find peer mentors for each student.* |

In this example, the Impact Team shared knowledge about the students 2–3 weeks after their arrival. The team determined short-term and longer-term support actions. The team will eventually use MTSS, but teachers want to keep them in their homerooms as much as possible so they develop strong connections. The Impact Team will revisit this every 6–8 weeks. The team started a Google Chat to maintain ongoing dialogue. They can share what is and is not working and allow the counselor, social worker, and others to communicate more responsively with the team.

## Personal Reflection

☐ What structures do you use to learn more about these students?

☐ Is your process asset-based? What is the evidence?

☐ Do you consistently meet as a cross-functional team?

☐ What are your next steps?

# EVIDENCE WALK PROTOCOL UNPACKED

Evidence walks (much like medical rounds) look closely at specific and predetermined practices central to formative assessment and related strategies that increase student ownership and agency. The purpose is twofold. They provide key evidence sources and a powerful feedback loop concerning systemic efforts. They provide 'assessment for learning' evidence.

The instructional leadership team supports school-level teams in determining evidence walk focus. Teams co-construct the 'evidence walk' success criteria to ensure transparency and clear communication.

Teams follow the three-step framework, Evidence - Analysis – Action (EAA) to

- Gather deep implementation of the formative process evidence
- Develop a shared understanding of effective formative practice
- Learn from others
- Distribute leadership
- Share decision-making about the school-wide learning focus
- Strengthen relational trust

## Evidence Walk Template

| EVIDENCE | ANALYSIS | ACTION |
|---|---|---|
| Gather evidence of learner agency using low inference notes:<br>• teacher observations<br>• student observations<br>• student voices<br>• the environment<br>• task rigor<br><br>What do we expect to observe:<br>• teachers co-constructing success criteria | • What does this evidence say about our core beliefs?<br>• How did the evidence illustrate the 4 sources of efficacy?<br>• What did you appreciate? Why?<br>• What do you wonder about? | • How will we sustain our assets?<br>• What will we stop doing?<br>• How can we improve? |

### Model of Success with Evidence Walks
### Petrides K-12 in Staten Island, NY

| | |
|---|---|
|  | The Petrides Middle School ILT learns as they debrief a student-led evidence walk. Students used the school's formative assessment focus to debrief their observations with the ILT and principal. They looked for evidence of 'assessment for learning'. Principal, Joanne Buckheit, facilitated this student focus group. To see this in action, view Video 7.1. |
|  | **Tip 7.2:** Learn more about this process by reading "Student-Led Instructional Debriefings" by principal Joanne Buckheit. |

### Team Reflection

• What do you notice about students' discourse?
• Were the students engaged? Why? How would you describe their level of engagement in this process?
• What is the general student confidence level? Why?
• How can their ILT use this evidence?

## Personal Reflection

- ☐ How is this similar to or different from other instructional rounds?

- ☐ Why are evidence walks important?

- ☐ How can you involve students and families in evidence walks?

# NUTSHELL

We aim to present a broader concept of evidence that stimulates team dialogue. Teams must triangulate data to gain a quality picture of student learning. An unrelenting focus on our students' assets (from socio-cultural and learning perspectives) can assist with breaking down systemic barriers. Relentlessly pursuing assets develops equitable partnerships with parents and students—if we seek their input and advice. If we want to advance Impact Team inquiry, teams need to grapple with puzzles of practice related to learner agency.

What relevant information informs teachers and students about the learning process? Specific evidence about learning is key to making informed collaborative decisions that center teams on the 'whole child'. Teams often base decisions on perspective, opinions, or outdated data.

These questions help teams recognize 'puzzles of practice':

- · What are our strengths? What led to our strengths? How can we sustain and learn from our strengths?
- · What are our greatest opportunities to advance learner agency? Why?
- · What are our families' and students' greatest assets?
- · What are the assets of our students who need the most support?
- · Who has been harmed the most by a lack of mastery? Why?
- · Who has not been harmed? Why?
- · How does a lack of mastery reveal itself in social and emotional well-being?

Once teams determine the 'puzzle of practice' and 'theory of action' they determine the evidence they will use to make informed decisions. When teams are engaged in data-driven decision making they need to hold each other accountable to their agreements and core beliefs (Chapter 3). Deeply ingrained beliefs guide organizational actions. They drive lived experiences and cultural identities, and they define our greater purposes. Our collective agreements ground us in who we strive to be.

## Team Reflection:

☐ What role does evidence play in your current teaming structures?

☐ What sources of evidence do teams use to define puzzles of practice?

☐ What sources of evidence do teams use to understand their inquiry's impact?

☐ Do you share decision-making with the people who are harmed the most?

## Equity Reflection:

☐ Are you considering diverse perspectives for inclusion?

☐ How do you leverage community assets in your data-driven decision-making?

☐ How can you partner with family and student experts, especially from historically underserved communities?

## CHECK-IN

Reflect on what and how you use evidence to inform teaching and learning. Add next steps to enhance collaborative practices.

| Evidence to Inform and Act | Not Yet | Sometimes | Always |
|---|---|---|---|
| We collect and analyze multiple qualitative and quantitative evidence sources to make informed decisions resulting in collective action. | | | |
| We triangulate evidence to understand impact. | | | |
| We use evidence-based practices that emphasize self-regulation and metacognition (thinking about thinking). | | | |
| We use asset-based pedagogies, Universal Design for Learning (UDL) and the formative practices when responding to evidence. | | | |
| We use MTSS to support our learners' academic, social, and emotional needs. | | | |
| We evaluate actions for impact. | | | |
| We use the AOE, Check-In, and Case Study Protocols to monitor progress. | | | |
| What's next? | | | |

**Chapter 7 Models of Success: Evidence to Inform and Act**

Overview: The videos in this chapter illustrate our thought partners using Impact Team Purposeful Protocols to guide inquiry cycles.

| | |
|---|---|
|  | **Video 7.2 Analysis of Student Work in Secondary:**<br><br>Model—AOE Team Meeting Protocol in Action: Analyzing Student Work, Lyons Township High School (LTHS), La Grange, Illinois.<br><br>Dr. Paul Bloomberg models peer facilitation using the AOE Team Meeting Protocol, Analyzing Student Work, for the LTHS World History Team. |
|  | **Video 7.3 Analysis of Student Work in Secondary:**<br><br>AOE Protocol in Action: Analysis of Student Work, LTHS, La Grange, Illinois<br><br>Dr. Paul Bloomberg coaches Jamie Bronuskas, chemistry peer facilitator at LTHS, the AOE Team Meeting Protocol with her Chemistry Team. |
|  | **Video 7.4 Analysis of Student Work in Elementary:**<br><br>AOE Protocol in Action: Analyzing Student Work, PS 9, Staten Island, NY.<br><br>The PS 9 second-grade team uses the AOE Protocol with their peer facilitator's guidance. |
|  | **Video 7.5 Analysis of Evidence in Middle School.**<br><br>The Impact Team Inquiry Blueprint in Action: Park Middle School, Kennewick, WA.<br><br>Learn from instructional and Impact Team coach, Gina Ferguson, about launching Impact Team inquiry with teams. |
|  | **Video 7.6: AOE Protocol in Elementary.**<br><br>Principal Testimonial, Julie Munn, Kelsey Norman Elementary, Joplin, Missouri<br><br>Principal Julie Munn, principal, talks about the ease of the AOE Protocol—Analyzing Student Work. |

# ACTIVATING A GUIDING COALITION

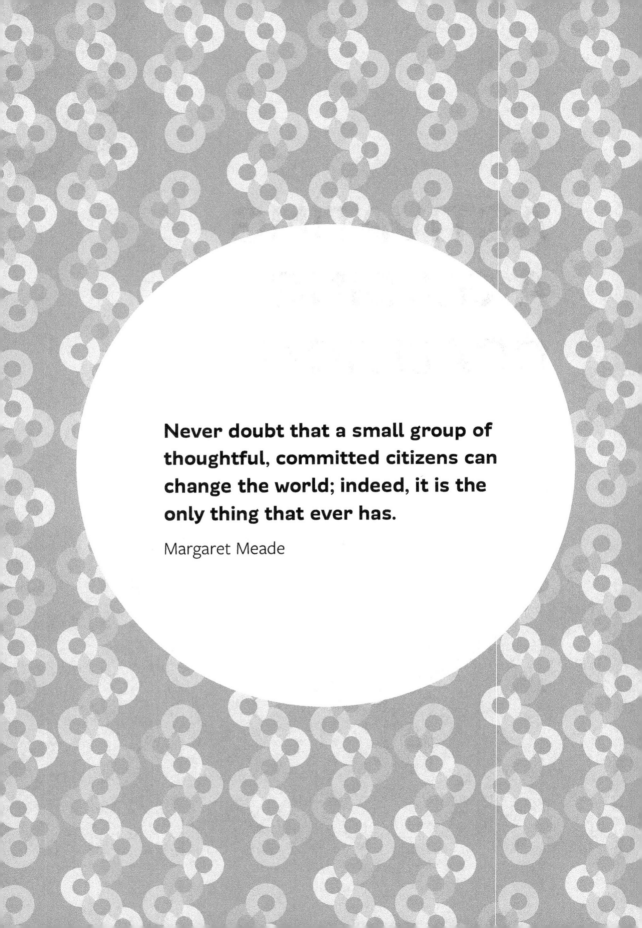

**Never doubt that a small group of thoughtful, committed citizens can change the world; indeed, it is the only thing that ever has.**

Margaret Meade

## Mastery Moment

Describe the best team leadership experience you've had when making a positive contribution to others. What conditions made this experience memorable?

# THE *WHAT:* ACTIVATING A GUIDING COALITION

Contrary to common belief, school leadership is not just the principal. All adults collectively commit to making a difference in the lives of all students. Effective educational leadership fosters working conditions in which professional growth, commitment, engagement, and a "constant spawning of leadership in others" thrive (Fullan 2010). Leadership develops collective capacity and builds student and teacher efficacy. Shared decision-making, collective interactions, trying things out, testing the waters, improving practices, reflecting on impact, and adjusting to improve practice fosters healthy transformation in schools. We call this *connected leadership*.

Any educator in the profession for over five years knows that all-school change takes time, perseverance, and unrelenting commitment. As Ringo Starr sang, *"It don't come easy, ya know, it doesn't come easy."* After working with schools in their change efforts and carefully observing, we learned the importance of internal collaborative expertise. Change happens from the inside out. We can only control ourselves. This realization frees us from top-down reforms that don't work.

A Guiding Coalition is a group of people working together to influence outcomes on school-wide goals. Guiding Coalitions are useful for accomplishing a broad range of goals that reach beyond the capacity of any individual or Impact Team. One of the most important aspects of a guiding coalition is its diversity. An effective coalition is composed of individuals from across the organization who contribute unique skills, experiences, perspectives and social networks in order to enable the most innovative strategies to come to fruition. Coalition members are a powerful, enthusiastic group of change agents who develop new strategies and put them into effect for school transformation (Kotter, 2012).

## WHY ESTABLISH A GUIDING COALITION?

Developing a guiding coalition, a change management strategy, leverages informal and formal social networks within your learning organization (Kotter, 2012). Collaborative leaders use this strategy because it makes practical sense. The individuals within guiding coalitions share their expertise, lived experiences, energy, and passion from across various areas: principal, ILT, model Impact Teams (PLCs), parent leader(s), other admin, department leads, union leadership, student leaders, lead paraprofessionals, other classified leadership, instructional and counseling leadership, and community leadership.

When school leaders partner with stakeholders to build a guiding coalition, they lead and learn from the inside out. Coalition members bring expertise, energy, and varied perspectives across multiple transformation domains. Peers respect their professionalism and ability to communicate and make quality connections, so they typically influence other stakeholders positively (social persuasion).

Building a guiding coalition aims to establish ownership and commitment by cultivating collaborative expertise. It advances targeted leadership, organizational, instructional, and programmatic strategies through collective decision-making to promote transformational and sustainable changes. The greater the diversity (ethnicity, gender, positional power, tenure, content, lived experiences, perspectives, and skills) of the coalition, the more respect and influence change agents will have for nurturing innovation, problem-solving, and collective efficacy.

# ADOPT A 'CONNECTED' WORLDVIEW

A *worldview* expresses a collection of background assumptions that are often subconscious. When we shift our worldview from seeing us as separate individuals to seeing ourselves as connected to each other, to nature, and to our world, we begin to shift our worldview (Allen, 2018). As we grow to understand and value other people's perspectives in a guiding coalition (and across our learning community) we begin to shift our worldview from separation to connection. Prioritizing relational literacy promotes seeing one another as truly "whole". By focusing on stakeholders' assets, we focus our energy on recognizing, valuing and leveraging the strengths, talents, experiences, and cultural backgrounds that every stakeholder brings to the learning community, rather than focusing solely on their deficits or challenges.

When our worldview shifts to connection, our personal and collective perspective changes, interdependence is obvious (Allen, 2018). Holding on to the belief that we are isolated individuals creates harm. If each stakeholder believes that they stand alone, then leading and acting in self-interest is a logical choice. This "self-interest mindset" by serving yourself first and holding on to power and resources, actually harms other people in your learning community. And when self-interest is unbridled, it harms others and the learning environment. Therefore, when we harm one person in our learning network, we harm ourselves as well.

However, when we see ourselves as interconnected, we understand that we are all a part of one living-learning ecosystem. Therefore, each person must recognize that they are part of that ecosystem and a part of what needs to be changed. By shifting our worldview to connection, we engage in collective problem-solving and shared decision-making because we understand the impact of our decisions on each person within our community (Allen, 2018). Teams prioritize approaches that mutually reinforce each other because they realize that sustainable change flows through quality connections. They understand that people support solutions they help design. When we prioritize relationships and connections as a viable approach to facilitate transformation, we create change that is sustainable and doesn't require power and resources to keep it in place.

## THE ANTIDOTE TO HIERARCHY

Connections shift hierarchies to networks and recognize feedback loops that give us information to adapt and thrive. Without a diverse guiding coalition, learning organizations rely solely on formal networks anchored in hierarchical operations. Formal structures grounded in a hierarchy often destroy organizational change rather than accelerate it. Hierarchy stifles reciprocal communication and threatens relational trust. Hierarchies can create a competitive, tense, and unfair environment for stakeholders. They can silence opinions and creativity. Authority bias, the tendency to overvalue opinions from the top of the hierarchy and undervalue opinions from the bottom, stifles innovation in its earliest stage (Clark, 2022). Teachers, families, and students don't hold much decision-making power regarding organizational goals. More and more, school transformation becomes a top-down endeavor.

Activating a guiding coalition is one antidote to the negative impact of authority bias. It reduces and balances typical power structures by grounding shared decision-making in collective agreements and core beliefs. With these key people at the table, they can nurture and develop models of success, refine communication, and bridge formal and informal social networks. Together, a coalition can transform hierarchical models into connected and collaborative models that sustain systemwide learner-centered efforts.

## SOCIAL NETWORKS PROPEL CHANGE

A formal network includes individuals possessing positional

power, such as a superintendent, director, coordinator, principal, or teacher. (See Chapter 3.) Formal network interactions stem from an industrial and typical hierarchical structure (Daly, 2010). These hierarchical structures dominate schools and systems across the globe. One person or multiple people at the top operates a hierarchy. Knowledge, expertise, and feedback flow downward to others with lower "formal" positions. This hierarchy typically creates an us-versus-them mentality, even though we are on the same team. In contrast, informal social networks include quality and quantity relationships (Daly, 2010). Informal social networks regularly and consistently share and build knowledge. For example, when I (Paul) was a 3rd grade teacher, five other teachers at my school (across grade levels) and I wanted to figure out how to better respond to our writers. We met together at a coffee shop every week to figure it out. We even met informally in my room during planning periods. This was happening as the rest of the school was doing in-depth learning on creating responsive reading mini-lessons. It wasn't that the schoolwide focus didn't meet our needs, we just had more pertinent puzzles of practice to figure out. When people learn together informally, communication is naturally reciprocal and grounded in relational trust. Figures 8.1 and 8.2 illustrate these concepts. This kind of informal learning is happening all the time. Since this is true, how can we leverage our informal social networks as a strategy to influence change? How can we nurture the conditions that anchor the learning that happens naturally in informal learning networks?

## Exploring a 'Work-Related Topic' Social Network

Figure 8.1 represents an organizational network map of a school district's informal social network and how they collaborate around **work-related topics**. These figures illustrate the quality and quantity of relational ties between school and district leaders around **work-related collaboration**. The white dots, or nodes, represent district leadership. The light gray nodes represent school leaders, including principals, deans, and assistant principals. When communication is reciprocated, the node becomes larger. If the node is central in the network, that person has more "knowledge power" within the network. In this case, you can see that district leaders hold most of the "knowledge" power within the system. You can also see that every leader connects to another, making relational ties quite dense. In this map, 36% of the existing collaboration ties were reciprocated, creating a dense informal social network. We can analyze this data to make inferences about the quality of relationships necessary to implement this district's professional learning goals. In this map, it is clear that leaders seek advice from each other on general work-related topics.

### Figure 8.1: Collaboration on 'Work-Related Topics" Social Network

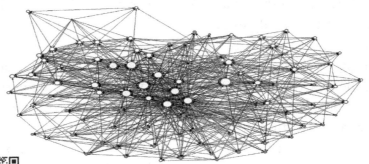

*Source*: Bloomberg, 2012.
Scan the QR code to view Figures 8.1 and 8.2 in color.

## Personal Reflection

☐ What do you notice about the network map connections?

☐ Why do you think this organization has such a dense network regarding collaboration on work-related topics? What does it say about their values and collective agreements?

☐ What are the benefits of reciprocal collaboration?

☐ Who holds the most positional power in this network? Why do you think that?

☐ How does positional power impact organizational learning? Why?

☐ What insight does this data give you about your leadership?

## Exploring a 'GRR Advice-Seeking' Social Network

In contrast, the organizational network map in Figure 8.2 represents how leaders "seek advice" from other leaders regarding the district professional learning goal, **implementing the gradual release of responsibility (GRR)**. It is a map of the **same** organization. This social network is extremely sparse, with few principals (gray nodes) turning to other principals or central office leaders for advice regarding the GRR initiative. All of the nodes in the top left corner represent individuals in the network who do not seek advice about GRR, nor does anyone seek them out. This map shows that 2 or 3 district leaders (white nodes) hold most of the knowledge power. Based on the node sizes, you see very little reciprocity. Why is that? The *'quality of our informal social networks matter'* when determining leadership strategies that ensure quality implementation of district or school professional learning goals.

**Figure 8.2: Advice-Seeking for 'GRR' Social Network**

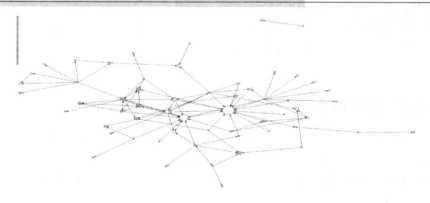

*Source*: Bloomberg, 2012.
Scan the QR code to view Figures 8.1 and 8.2 in color.

## Personal Reflection

☐ What do you notice about the 'GRR' network map connections?

☐ Who holds the most positional power? Why do you think that?

☐ Why is the advice-seeking social network so sparse? Why do you think that? (The district has been implementing 'GRR' for 3 years.)

☐ How does positional power impact organizational learning in this map? Why?

☐ How is this map similar to or different from the other? Why are the maps so different even though they come from the same organization?

☐ Why was the 'work-related topic' network more dense than the 'GRR' network?

☐ What role do communication, relational trust, and sense of belonging play in the quality of professional social networks?

☐ What insight does this data give you about your leadership?

**Tip 8.1:** Learn more about organizational network mapping and our partnership with Professor Alan Daly in video 8.1.

## BUILDING A GUIDING COALITION

Guiding coalitions reflect informal and formal social networks that drive systemic learning. Dennis Goin, executive engagement leader of Kotter International, notes two essential factors: *diversity* and *behavior* (Kotter, Inc., 2022).

Your guiding coalition should reflect the *diversity* of your school community. Individual characteristics should vary in skills, lived experiences, perspectives, knowledge and the ability to connect with others in healthy ways. The coalition should include representatives from various levels of the organization, different departments or functions, and individuals with different expertise including parent leaders, classified leaders and your ILT. This diversity ensures that a wide range of perspectives and insights are considered during the change process.

*Behavior* is an essential ingredient to the coalition's success. Avoid deficit-minded individuals as much as possible. Focus on organizational strengths and center your team on rich human assets. The most successful coalitions have a balance of introverts and extroverts, as well as conventional and unconventional thinkers. We want to embrace unconventional thinking and understand a wide range of perspectives, even though they may not align with traditional, formal leadership. The team must embody the school's shared agreements and core beliefs to align with the organizational mission. (See Chapter 3.) Quality implementation advances collaborative inquiry by adopting and executing key strategies (leadership, organizational, instructional, and programmatic) that lead to mastery experiences for all stakeholders.

## Personal Reflection

☐ How is the "guiding coalition" approach similar to or different from other change management strategies?

☐ How would your ILT cultivate a guiding coalition to maximize and realize school improvement goals?

☐ What role will diversity and an asset-centered mindset play in your coalition?

☐ What stakeholders will compose your guiding coalition? Why?

# THE *WHY:* RESEARCH AND REASONS

There is a strong causal relationship between the following four collaborative leadership components: 1) instructional leadership, 2) teacher collaboration, 3) teacher efficacy beliefs, and 4) student achievement (Goddard et al., 2015). The latter leadership components interact and align a systemic process that ensures schoolwide progress.

## REASON 1: COLLABORATIVE INQUIRY FOSTERS COLLECTIVE EFFICACY.

Collaborative learning and leading build the belief that the members of the team have the expertise to do great things. When teachers share responsibility, they feel empowered. When they feel empowered, they feel confident they can make a difference. When they believe they can make a difference, they do! These beliefs lead to mastery experiences that build collective efficacy and serve as success models for others (Eells, 2011).

## REASON 2: STRONG CONNECTIONS SUPPORT PROBLEM-SOLVING.

When learning communities value relational literacy they prioritize and practice healthy ways of connecting and collaborating. They practice active listening to ensure each member is truly heard. "Social networks with strong ties can facilitate diffusion of innovation, transfer of complex information, and increased problem-solving. Strong social networks increase individual and organizational performance" (Coburn et al., 2019, p. 33).

## REASON 3: FOCUSING ON PROGRESS IMPROVES THE QUALITY OF LEARNING.

Engaging all teachers relentlessly and collaboratively in learning reaps great rewards (Fullan & Quinn, 2016). Changing the paradigm from accountability (test scores) to ensuring *progress* empowers teachers to be responsive to student learning. It is key to a collective that makes a difference. "The more willing principals are to spread leadership around, the better for the students" (Harvey & Holland, 2012).

## REASON 4: COLLABORATIVE INQUIRY IMPROVES THE QUALITY OF TEACHING.

Learning, taking action, analyzing impact, and taking collective action improves the learning lives of students. Teacher collaboration quality can positively or negatively influence teaching quality and student achievement (Ronfeldt et al., 2015). Accepting their role as key leaders and contributors to student success, teachers identify puzzles of practice, successes, and challenges. They continuously engage in inquiry cycles, developing effective practices.

## REASON 5: COLLABORATION BUILDS AND SUSTAINS COLLECTIVE COMMITMENT.

Cultivating a collaborative culture grounded in shared purpose leads to ongoing learning experiences that present challenges, successes, dilemmas, frustrations, and productive struggle. But it ultimately results in improved student learning. Teachers become leaders, leaders become learners, and change in practice evolves when organizations operate from a strengths-based mindset. These mastery experiences, interspersed with challenges and failures, strengthen collective resolve to make a difference for all students: the bedrock belief of a school.

School improvement is not a one-person band. "In fact, if test scores are any indication, the more willing principals are to spread leadership around, the better for students. . . . Principals may be relieved to find out, moreover, that their authority does not wane as others' waxes. Clearly, school leadership is not a zero-sum game"

(Harvey & Holland, 2012). We can only reach our true potential through collaboration. However, the collaborative, interdependent shift requires time and effort. Develop a diverse guiding coalition to achieve long, deep, and sustainable change.

# THE HOW: FORMING AND SUSTAINING IMPACT TEAMS

Building capacity with the Impact Team Model requires systems to consider the relationship between informal and formal networks. Promoting and refining strong, quality personal and learning connections anchored in relational trust ensures quality information sharing and building. The Impact Team implementation model leverages the four sources of efficacy and the enabling conditions that foster collective efficacy. (Chapter 2) It builds collaborative expertise of key practices related to inquiry. Educators build their collaborative expertise through deliberate practice that results in mastery experiences for every member. Teams become models for stakeholders across the learning organization.

If we have learned anything from the past two decades of school reform, attempting to change all schools in one fatal swoop carries significant risks. Implementing change takes tremendous resources regarding time and people, and schools need more resources to ensure fidelity. When things go awry, the practice often results in something other than the advertised outcomes. Teachers become disenchanted and back away. "This too shall pass," and it does, and the initiative leaves a bad taste. To prevent this negative experience, we use "strategic resourcing" to ensure success (Viviane Robinson 2011). That is, we deal with reality, wisely using available resources to support changes.

**Tip 8.2:** Read more about supporting lasting change in schools in Peter DeWitt's, *Instructional Leadership:*

*Creating Practice Out of Theory*. Small manageable changes over time make all the difference.

# PRINCIPAL AS LEAD LEARNER

The principal and ILT drive the Impact Team guiding coalition. Without the principal's unwavering commitment to the Impact Team Model, pockets of teachers may not embrace best practices or key processes, resulting in a fragmented implementation.

Principals must understand the enabling conditions to strengthen collective efficacy, how efficacy is related to student-centered learning, and how to strengthen self-efficacy for students, teachers, and family-caregivers. With that commitment comes a call to action and a commitment to model the formative assessment core practices by walking the talk.

Robinson, Lloyd, & Rowe (2008) did a meta-analysis of about 30 studies on educational leadership and were able to sort 199 surveyed leadership measurements into five leadership dimensions and calculate the effect size for each dimension. They grouped 199 measured leadership aspects into five categories and calculated how much each category influenced student outcomes. This influence is measured as an "effect size." An effect size of 0.2 is small, 0.4 is moderate, and 0.6 and higher is large.

| Leadership Dimensions | Effect Size |
|---|---|
| 1. Establishing goals and expectations | .42 |
| 2. Resourcing strategically | .31 |
| 3. Ensuring quality teaching | .42 |
| 4. Leading teacher learning and development | .84 |
| 5. Ensuring a safe and orderly environment | .27 |

Robinson's book, *Student-Centered Leadership* (2011), clarifies how to set clear goals for student learning. It includes resources and offers strategies for planning, coordinating, and monitoring achievement. Robinson's five dimensions are interdependent and guide instructional leadership teams and guiding coalition work. Note dimension four; this dimension yields the highest effect. The principal in partnership with the ILT (and trained ITM peer facilitators) leads and facilitates Impact Team inquiry work across the school. Leaders make the most impact on student learning by promoting and participating in teachers' professional learning and development.

## Personal Reflection

- ☐ How much time is dedicated to the five student-centered leadership dimensions?

- ☐ What are your strengths and biggest opportunities for growth?

**Tip 8.3**: Michael McDowell, in his book *The Lead Learner*, describes a new model of educational leadership that ensures core academic content and 21st-century skill growth for all students (2018). With practical examples, stories from the field, and numerous activities and reflective questions, his insightful book takes you step-by-step through the work of the learning leader. It helps you meet the unique learning needs of staff and students to get the biggest impact. He describes how to:
- ensure clarity in strategic planning,
- establish system coherence,
- enact systemwide capacity-building processes, and
- craft your personal leadership skills.

## ADVANCE CONNECTED LEADERSHIP

Connected leadership is crucial for establishing a guiding coalition as it fosters a sense of ownership, shared vision, and values the diverse expertise among team members. Hierarchical methods of command and control management styles, which leaders so often fall back on in times of stress (or because they don't have an alternative approach to rely on) usually lead to anything but positive relationships anchored in relational trust and belonging (Marsh, 2019).

A connected leader is someone with high levels of self-awareness, someone who comes across as human, someone who is not afraid to be vulnerable. A connected leader collaborates with their team and encourages honest dialogue and input from them in return. A connected leader is someone who will elevate people to be the best version of themselves (Marsh, 2019).

By valuing input from various stakeholders and facilitating open communication, connected leaders create a more inclusive and innovative environment where individuals are empowered to contribute their unique perspectives. This approach not only strengthens the quality of decision-making and problem-solving within the coalition but also cultivates a stronger commitment to the collective goals, ultimately enhancing the coalition's ability to navigate complex challenges and drive meaningful change. Consider these five elements as you harness the power of your guiding coalition to strengthen school improvement goals.

1. Ensure diverse expertise

2. Nurture relational trust

3. Co-design clear goals

4. Establish credibility

5. Organize-communicate for collective action

## 1. Ensure Diverse Expertise

Guiding coalitions represent different points of view and expertise derived from the lived experiences, and it requires specialized expertise from the most impacted areas in your system. The coalition embodies a "solution-focused mindset" to solve puzzles of practice that harm students and families. Inviting one or two PLCs to become "model" Impact Teams supports the mission of building collaborative expertise through collaborative inquiry. Diverse expertise comes from across your system: family and caregivers, paraprofessionals, counselors and social workers, special educators, multilingual learners, and others. Most important, the guiding coalition should represent the demographics of the community.

## 2. Nurture Relational Trust

Relational trust is the glue that sticks members of an organization together. Talking about the reality of trust in your system is crucial. Transparency, honesty, and quality planning nurture an atmosphere of relational trust. Ensuring "everyone is honored and feels welcome, not by accident, but by design" is foundational. Those in roles of traditionally held power may need to "let go of who we are so we can become who we need to be" (Cobb & Krownapple, 2019, p. 30). Building trust takes time and effort. Use practical tools and advice to strengthen relational trust in your system. (See Chapter 2 and the online appendix)

## 3. Co-design Clear Goals

Guiding coalitions use design thinking to develop goals. This process ensures that the coalition is solution-focused and human-centered. Design thinking is also an extension of innovation. Collective decision-making, grounded in organizational collective agreements and core values, ensures goal consensus. Review the Design Thinking planning process to create systemic goals. (See Chapter 4.)

## 4. Establish Credibility

Include members with solid reputations within the organization. Guiding coalition members may not represent our dominant cultural values. Their perspective is essential for innovation and responsiveness to community needs. Recruiting new members with fresh eyes provides a different perspective, and they can establish credibility over time. Credibility is essential when creating commitment and goal consensus.

## 5. Organize and Communicate for Collective Action

Guiding coalition members need organizational and communication skills to manage the details and logistics of the change process. ILTs must communicate and listen effectively within the coalition and the wider organization. Ensuring community agreements through shared decision-making is essential to this team's success. Read more about creating collective agreements in Chapter 3. Guiding coalitions aim to cultivate commitment and ownership. Their attempt to recruit more Impact Teams by highlighting short-term wins, mastery experiences and positive impact.

Equally important to identifying the messages you want to communicate out to your broader learning community is determining the mode that will be used to communicate your message. Be sure you have the appropriate channels in place to communicate your intentions, plans, and activities to everyone in your school community; this is critical to ensure that everyone is rowing in the same direction. (ie: website, texting service, social media channels, online portal that is accessible to staff and parents, back to school night, curriculum nights, staff meetings, school newsletters, local news, etc.).

## Example Communication Guidelines

| Stakeholder Target Audience | Targeted Message Based on Role | Communication Channels |
|---|---|---|
| **Example: Families** | *Our school is investing resources and professional learning time in teaching your child how to self-assess and set and monitor their learning goals. These practices have the greatest potential to accelerate learning. We would like to share this vision with you and get your advice on how best to implement this.* | *• Parent-Teacher Meetings*<br>*• Online Parent Portal*<br>*• Social Media*<br>*• Calls by Parent Coordinator*<br>*• School Website* |

| Stakeholder Target Audience | Targeted Message Based on Role | Communication Channels |
|---|---|---|
| **Example: Students** | *Student Council: Our school is investing learning time in teaching you how to set and monitor your learning goals. Our team would like to get your perspective as we create a school-wide plan. You are invited too....* | • *Online Student Council Chat*<br>• *Student Council Email*<br>• *Student Council Meeting* |
| **Faculty (classified and certificated)** | | |
| **District** | | |
| **School Board** | | |
| **Community Members** | | |

Notice the message in the example above. The message is personalized based on the targeted audience. For relational trust to flourish, communication has to be in a state of continuous improvement. All systems need to continuously work on quality communication that leads to higher levels of relational trust.

## Personal Reflection

What informal learning networks "live" in your school? What formal learning networks "live" in your school? How can you use your formal and informal social networks to influence more stakeholders?

# FORMING A GUIDING COALITION

The composition of a guiding coalition is crucial for the success of change efforts. The principal, in partnership with their ILT, invites diverse stakeholders to be a part of the guiding coalition. The members represent the school's supported demographics. Here are some key considerations for determining who should be in a guiding coalition to make change:

- **Diverse Representation:** Coalition membership should reflect the ethnic diversity of your school and system. The coalition should also include representatives from various levels of the organization, different departments or functions, and individuals with different expertise including parent leaders, classified leaders and your ILT. This diversity ensures that a wide range of perspectives and insights are considered during the change process.
- **Leadership Support:** It's essential to have key leaders on board, including the principal, the ILT and other teachers and parent leaders who can influence and drive change across the organization. Their support and commitment lend credibility and resources to the initiative.
- **Change Champions:** Identify individuals who are enthusiastic about school improvement and have a track record of successfully implementing similar initiatives. These change champions can inspire and motivate others to embrace the change.
- **Subject Matter Experts:** Include individuals who possess expertise related to the change initiative. Their knowledge will be valuable in shaping the strategy and making informed decisions.
- **Frontline Employees:** Involve stakeholders who are directly affected by the change on a day-to-day basis. Their input provides insights into potential challenges and practical considerations that might arise during implementation.

- **Cross-Functional Collaboration:** Ensure that the coalition members come from different functional areas within the organization. This promotes collaboration and helps avoid a siloed approach to change.
- **Influencers:** Identify individuals who have informal influence within the organization. They may not hold formal leadership positions but are respected and trusted by their peers, making them effective advocates for change.
- **Stakeholder Representation:** Include representatives from stakeholder groups that will be impacted by the change including students and parent leaders. Their input helps ensure that all perspectives are considered and valued.
- **Innovation Drivers:** Include individuals who are known for their innovative thinking and willingness to explore new ideas. They can contribute creative solutions to challenges that arise during the change process.
- **Communication Skills:** Choose individuals who are effective communicators and can convey the rationale behind the change, address concerns, and keep the organization informed throughout the process.
- **Resilience:** Change efforts can face resistance and setbacks. Members of the guiding coalition should have the resilience and determination to navigate challenges and keep the initiative on track.
- **Credibility:** Members of the coalition should have a certain level of credibility and respect within the organization. Their involvement lends legitimacy to the change effort.
- **Inclusivity:** Ensure that the coalition is representative of the organization's diversity in terms of gender, ethnicity, age, and other dimensions.
- **Commitment:** Coalition members should be committed to the long-term success of the change initiative. This requires a willingness to invest time, effort, and resources into the process.

Remember that the specific composition of the guiding coalition will vary based on the nature of the change, the organization's culture, and the challenges involved. Regular communication, collaboration, and a shared sense of purpose among coalition members are essential for successfully leading change within an organization.

**Bluewave Middle School Example:**

Bluewave Middle School launched Impact Teams with their ILT. Their ILT attended the Impact Team foundational professional learning and then assessed their system using the Impact Team Pre-Assessment. They used the "Review Tool Protocol" to identify their strengths and biggest opportunities for improvement. Then, they determined what stakeholders they wanted to invite to the coalition to launch Impact Teams schoolwide.

Figure 8.3 illustrates the membership of Bluewave Middle's guiding coalition. Notice the 'connected leadership' network structure of the guiding coalition (this kind of network structure balances traditional power structures). In connected systems, information flows freely and transparently, communication is reciprocated and the guiding coalition members co-construct collective agreements and core values that ground their collective decision-making.

**Figure 8.3: Bluewave Middle Guiding Coalition Members**

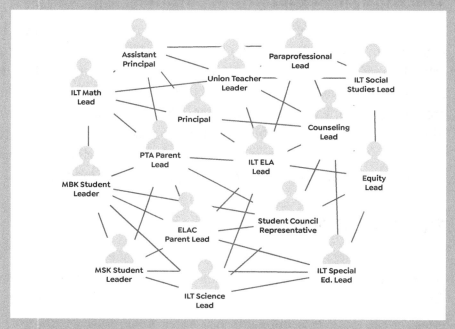

## The Role of the ILT

The instructional leadership team (ILT) is core to the development of a guiding coalition. The ILT in a school plays a pivotal role in driving educational excellence and fostering a culture of continuous improvement. Comprising administrators, Impact Team peer facilitators (grade level, course alike or department leads), instructional, counseling specialists, and lead paraprofessionals, this team collaboratively develops, executes and monitors schoolwide continuous improvement goals.

The ILT uses the Impact Team pre-assessment results to make decisions about the strategic planning for 'assessment for learning' and Impact Team implementation. In addition, they analyze data, identify areas for growth, facilitate Impact Teams (PLCs), and offer support to educators, ensuring alignment with educational goals and standards. Through their guidance and expertise, the instructional leadership team empowers teachers, staff and families, facilitates meaningful learning experiences, and contributes to overall school continuous improvement efforts. They also are instrumental in determining membership of the guiding coalition.

## The Role of Model Impact Teams

A school's PLCs provide a perfect structure for capacity building. Model Impact Teams (PLCs) are important members of a school's guiding coalition. Therefore, ILTs invite 1-2 Impact Teams (PLCs) to serve as models of success for other teams. This action creates opportunities for vicarious learning experiences for new PLCs being trained in key impact team processes. The model teams can coach and provide peer support to build capacity with new teams and provide support for teams engaged in the model.

## The Role of Parent Leaders

Parent leaders and community leaders are vital members of a school's guiding coalition. Creating authentic partnerships with families is critical when committing to equitable family engagement. This requires an intentional, long-term effort to change unconscious perceptions, beliefs, and practices that live in traditional school settings. "These efforts are most effective when *student progress* is perceived by both families and school staff as a *shared responsibility*, underscored by mutual respect" (SEDL & US Department of Education, 2013). Educate school staff about cultural responsiveness and explore key concepts, such as implicit bias and identity (Richards et al., 2007) to ensure quality collaboration when engaged in collective decision making. If we want to authentically partner with families, we must ask for their advice and honor their lived experience as a vital source of knowledge that can benefit organizational learning. Include family representatives when engaging in knowledge building and shared decision making who reflect the diversity of the student body; this approach will ensure that family engagement is not a top-down initiative. Creating time for reciprocal dialogue with families is an important ingredient in building a shared language of learning.

**Tip 8.4**: To learn more about engaging with families, particularly those who have been marginalized, refer to Chapter 2 of *Amplify Learner Voice through Culturally Responsive and Sustaining Assessment* by The Core Collaborative Network authors. The authors share interview questions, personal vignettes, and communication examples.

## The Role of Specialized Support

Every school has specialized support people or support teams that offer differentiated support based on the schools personalized needs. (ie: SEL Team, Equity Team, Counselors, Reading Specialists, Social Workers, Math Coach, etc). This specialized expertise is necessary for Impact Team implementation, therefore, it is critical for the ILT to think of the specialized support they need when determining guiding coalition membership.

# LAUNCHING THE IMPACT TEAM GUIDING COALITION

After committing to learning and practicing the Impact Team Model, begin to review current practices. Assess the key ITM competencies using the Impact Team pre-assessment that you can access in Tip 8.5. Consider using the Review Tool to analyze the assessment results (see Figure 8.4).

 **Tip 8.5**: Access the Impact Team Pre-Assessment in the online appendix to assess strengths and opportunities, then determine the next steps.

**Figure 8.4: Review Tool Protocol**

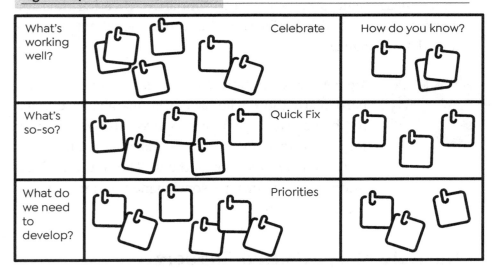

A guiding coalition created these baseline evidence statements based on their ITM pre-assessment:

- Educators are familiar with the "assessment for learning (A4L) competencies" anchored in Danielson 3-D.
- More than 70% of teachers reported that they needed to develop A4L practices in their classrooms.
- We have no evidence that families/caregivers understand A4L

practices. We will need to gather this evidence.

- We have no evidence students feel confident about formative assessment. We will need to survey students.
- Most families need clarification about how formative assessment supports students' personal lives and success in college and careers. Again, we need more data to be sure this is accurate.
- Teams have time weekly to collaborate in PLCs using the ITM.
- The curriculum is currently not culturally responsive and lacks coherence.
- Trust survey results indicate that we need to strengthen relational trust with staff and students. We need a more comprehensive sample for families and caregivers since only 30% took the survey.
- An internal survey reported that most teachers have little understanding of collaborative inquiry.

## Personal Reflection

☐ What do you notice about these baseline evidence statements?

☐ How might this information be used? Why?

☐ How will this information help the guiding coalition design goals?

☐ How are you gathering data at the onset of a new systemic goal in your organization?

☐ How are you gathering data to monitor progress or systemic goals?

## THE POWER OF PEER FACILITATION

Impact Teams lead from within. They select trained peer facilitators to guide inquiry, investigation, and collaborative learning. In our model, peer facilitators receive additional training in core

Impact Team protocols peer facilitation. Facilitators model investigative practice, risk-taking, and knowledge sharing. "Peer-facilitators are uniquely positioned to model a leap of faith, frame the work as an investigation, help the group stick with it, and guide protocol used as a full participant in the inquiry process" (Gallimore et al., 2009). They guide colleagues and learn with them, trying out lessons, partnering with students, and focusing on understanding their impact, ensuring the team realizes its full, collective potential. The facilitator:

- establishes roles
- ensures collective agreements are followed
- facilitates the meeting using purposeful protocols
- implements active listening, clear, concise summarization, and strengthening empathy
- adheres to time frames, topics, and outcomes
- advances prompt robust dialogue and discourse through appreciative inquiry
- stimulates knowledge sharing and new learning.

At least four times a year, peer facilitators need job-embedded support to facilitate team meetings. The best job-embedded coaching involves solving "peer facilitation" practice puzzles that facilitators often deal with. Typically peer facilitators are also members of the ILT so they can support each other during regular ILT meetings.

 **Tip 8.6**: See the online appendix for peer facilitator scaffolds and facilitation moves that take your teams from good to great.

# THE GRADUAL RELEASE OF RESPONSIBILITY

The gradual release model works through modeling, practice, and feedback. This is an execution-as-learning process. Teams learn protocols as needed through coaching and modeling. This authentic and organic implementation process contextually develops various skills and knowledge.

- Facilitate a meeting using the EAA framework
- Enhance formative assessment in the class
- Use protocols for specific purposes
- Determine and use quality evidence
- Do a critical analysis of the student learning root cause
- Determine the highest impact strategies directly related to root cause(s)
- Understand the impact of collective action

Impact Team coaches gradually release the facilitation of the Impact Team processes and structures to other members. During the gradual release, an Impact Team coach partners directly with a model team, the principal, and the peer facilitator. They co-design a blueprint for inquiry, develop an action theory, and use purposeful protocols that bring inquiry to life. Teams, in partnership with their coach, envision success before they begin, and then benchmark their inquiry. Throughout four or five meetings or classroom observations, the principal, peer facilitator, and team learn how to use the protocols.

## CREATING COLLABORATIVE EXPERTISE

The guiding coalition functions as the brain of a successful Impact Team. It leverages formal and informal social networks, ensuring that knowledge sharing and building is an interdependent, active sport. The guiding coalition is an accountable, diverse group bound by opportunity, strategy, and collective action (Kotter, Inc., 2018). They co-design a strategic implementation plan grounded in collective agreements and core values, invite new teams, remove barriers to quality implementation, generate short-term mastery moments, and refine and sustain school improvement efforts. They make learning sticky.

It is not a perfect process; it is a learning process. But, as with all learning, deliberate practice with feedback enables systems to move from "co-blab-or-ating" to forming quality learning partnerships. They grow collaborative expertise and build a culture of efficacy and agency for absolutely every learner in the system.

## Leveraging Your Personal Learning Network

When developing collaborative expertise, it is important for all learning community members to explore their personal, informal, social network when establishing a guiding coalition. Professor Alan Daly, a global social network theory and educational change researcher, designed the following exercise. It helps us understand the power of our informal social networks when implementing Impact Teams or other initiatives.

We all live in an ecosystem of relationships that enable us to accomplish tasks with varying degrees of success. In this exercise, consider the individuals connected to your system-wide goals and work. The concentric circles symbolize groups of individuals categorized by their significance in assisting you to achieve your goals. Write the names of people you work with based on how "close" they are to you in the three circles.

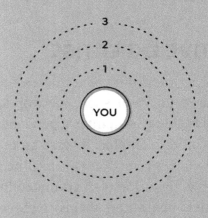

1. "Closest" means that you turn to them regularly, and they provide you with important resources, knowledge, information, and expertise. Put their names on the inner circle (Circle #1).

2. "Somewhat close" means you interact with them, but not often. Put their names on the middle circle (Circle #2).

3. "Not very close at all" means the interaction may not occur often, and it may be relatively superficial. Put their names on the outermost circle (Circle #3).

Now consider your map. Reflect on the following questions.

· What did you learn from this exercise?

· What would happen if you connected two people to your learning network?

· How does this exercise impact your guiding coalition membership?

· How can your personal network support your team and/or system in realizing their goal?

· What is the relationship between informal and formal social networks in your organization?

· How would you use this exercise with stakeholders? Why?

· How can we use our existing social networks to maximize organizational learning?

## Fostering Self-Empowerment

Harnessing the power of collaborative inquiry to promote actions that strengthen human connection, self-regulation and metacognition fosters self-efficacy and empowerment for all. Self-empowerment means consciously deciding to take charge of your destiny. It involves making positive choices, taking action to advance learning, and feeling confident in your ability to execute decisions while contributing positively to others. This is the aim of the Impact Team Model for absolutely every learner in the system. (And, yes, we are all learners.)

## NUTSHELL

Educators are professional learners. We like to learn, and we know how. The complexity of our profession requires constant learning to meet the challenging needs of our students. However, putting our new learning into practice is where the rubber meets the road, and where we encounter implementation challenges. Creating and sustaining a guiding coalition to build collaborative expertise is foundational. Building a diverse coalition helps everyone learn more.

## Team Reflection

☐ What is a guiding coalition? Why do they matter to the ITM?

☐ How can informal learning networks be used to build learning capacity?

☐ Why is it important to balance traditional power structures within our schools?

☐ Who would you invite to join the ITM guiding coalition? Why?

☐ What key information will you use to create a quality implementation plan?

## Equity Reflection:

☐ In what ways have our experiences with schooling created blind spots, biases, or perspectives that make it hard to reflect, change, and see new possibilities?

☐ How can our ITM model be more democratic and have equity-centered leadership?

# CHECK-IN

Use the checklist to activate a guiding coalition and to determine strengths and next steps.

| Action Steps | Not Yet | In Progress | Next Steps |
|---|---|---|---|
| **Collective Leadership** | | | |
| Our principal commits to enhancing learning assessment via collaborative inquiry. | | | |
| Our ILT demonstrates and values vulnerability to strengthen relational trust. | | | |
| Our ILT commits to activating change through collaborative inquiry. | | | |
| Our ILT uses evidence to identify strengths and determine the greatest opportunities to advance A4L through collaborative inquiry. | | | |
| Our ILT values diverse ideas to solve practice puzzles | | | |
| Our community co-constructs school goals through shared decision-making. | | | |
| **Activating a Guiding Coalition** | | | |
| ILT invites stakeholders to join the Impact Team guiding coalition. (The ILT lies at the heart of the guiding coalition.) | | | |

| Action Steps | Not Yet | In Progress | Next Steps |
|---|---|---|---|
| **Activating a Guiding Coalition continued** | | | |
| Our guiding coalition nurtures and values diversity in content expertise, function, ethnicity, organizational roles, and more. | | | |
| Our guiding coalition embodies an asset-centered and inquiry mindset. | | | |
| Model Impact Teams join the guiding coalition with other key stakeholders (department chairs, grade-level leads, social workers, and more). | | | |
| Family and student stakeholders are valued members of our guiding coalition. | | | |
| **Assessment for Learning** | | | |
| Our Impact Teams commit to advancing student ownership and agency. | | | |
| Our guiding coalition and current PLCs assess learning assessment quality. | | | |
| Our guiding coalition determines strengths and greatest opportunities to grow quality formative assessment across the school. | | | |
| Our school-based Impact Teams-PLCs share and grow knowledge about "assessment for learning" to ensure quality implementation. | | | |

| Action Steps | Not Yet | In Progress | Next Steps |
|---|---|---|---|
| **Collaborative Inquiry** | | | |
| Our guiding coalition engages in collaborative inquiry to learn the tenets of design thinking. | | | |
| Our school uses the gradual release of responsibility to explain and model key Impact Team processes. | | | |
| Our teams meet weekly for at least 45 minutes. | | | |
| Our teams benchmark and share their inquiry at least 2-3 times yearly to promote knowledge sharing and building. | | | |
| The ILT uses team time to advance peer facilitation. Each Impact Team has a trained peer facilitator. | | | |
| Our Impact Teams receive feedback on our collaborative practices and our inquiry cycle. | | | |
| What's Next? | | | |

**Models of Success: Video Descriptions**

**Chapter 8: Activating a Guiding Coalition**

Overview: The videos in this chapter illustrate the power of the Model Teams Approach in building Impact Team Capacity.

| | |
|---|---|
| | **Video 8.2:**<br>Cheryle Lerch, district FBISD leader in Sugar Land, TX, gives leaders a few tips for quality Impact Team implementation |
| | **Video 8.3:**<br>The Model Team Approach, Lyons Township High School (LTHS), La Grange, Illinois<br>Dr. Brian Waterman, principal of LTHS, provides his perspective on launching Model Impact Teams. |
| | **Video 8.4:**<br>Impact Team Quality Implementation, Core Collaborative Learning Network, Pittsburgh, KS<br>Sarah Stevens, executive director of quality implementation for Core Collaborative Learning, gives her perspective and tips for quality ITM implementation. |
| | **Video 8.5**<br>Teacher and Principal Testimonials, Reeds Spring School District, Missouri<br>Susi Mauldin, sixth-grade communication arts teacher, talks about the impact of the ITM. |
| | **Video 8.6**<br>Impact Team Implementation Tips, PS 9, Staten Island, NY<br>PS 9 Impact Team leaders, Nicole Hughes and Stephanie Bargone, give teacher teams a few Impact Team implementation tips. |

|  | **Video 8.7:**<br><br>The Model Team Approach, East Central BOCES, Limon, Colorado<br><br>Sharon Daxton-Vorce, Impact Team coach and coordinator of professional learning for the EC BOCES at the time of this video, discusses how their team built capacity with the Model Team Approach. |
|---|---|
|  | **Video 8.8:**<br><br>Teaching and Learning Coach, Kelsey Norman Elementary, Joplin, Missouri<br><br>Hope Strasser, teaching and learning coach, discusses how collaboration supports classroom clarity. |

# OUR
# INVITATION

# AN INVITATION TO YOU

This book has been a labor of love, and, as with any labor of love, we hope that it has an impact far beyond our reach. We aimed to provide the ideas, structures, processes, and examples necessary to launch, sustain, or refine your journey in building a culture of efficacy to advance learner agency.

Change agents in any context require knowledge, skills, and a true desire to have an impact. We hope this book complemented the assets you brought and challenged your previous thinking and assumptions. However, knowledge and desire without taking action won't lead us to our desired destination.

So now is the time for action!

Consider these 10 factors to assist you on your Impact Team journey.

> **1. Be vulnerable.** It took two authors, three contributors, and scores of educators, students, and families to create what you see here.

> **2. Actively listen.** To build quality learning partnerships, we have to listen to understand. Our learners can use funds of knowledge as superpowers.

> **3. Practice empathy.** Empathy is key to understanding our shared humanity. It allows us to understand what drives others' actions. When we practice empathy, we position ourselves to connect with and understand others—and ourselves.

> **4. Lean into identity.** Cultural identity impacts learning. Race, social class, gender, language, sexual orientation, nationality, religion, and ability influence education. Our learners

need mirrors that reflect the greatness of their communities. They also need windows into the world, allowing them to connect across cultures.

**5. Balance power.** The more power you share with learners, the more agency they will have. Build off of strengths and involve students in setting ambitious, relevant goals. (This goes for teachers and families too.)

**6. Lead by example.** Leading by example makes a powerful statement. Immerse yourself in inquiry and formative assessment. Be open and honest about what and how you learn. If you lead by example, you can inspire innovation and change.

**7. Educate.** Partner up with others, and start your inquiry group. Begin a book club to reflect on the big ideas this book presents.

**8. Be bold.** Enhance current practice. Take a risk and try something new. Don't expect perfection; there is no such thing.

**9. Raise awareness.** Social media has revolutionized communication. It is a powerful educational tool. Whatever platform you choose, connect with individuals and networks that share the same values and goals. Write a blog or create a video with your students. Please share what you are doing with others so they can learn vicariously through you. Join our "Leading Impact Teams" Facebook Group.

**10. Reflect.** Reflect on the conditions and mastery experiences that foster collective efficacy, where all learners thrive. Your network's impact is what matters most.

*Source:* Adapted from Bloomberg et al. (2022). *Amplify learner voice through culturally responsive and sustaining assessment.* Mimi and Todd Press. Copyright 2022.

# OUR AGREEMENTS

We wrote these agreements to inspire you. We hope they will help your network to recommit to our collective cause of strengthening learner efficacy and agency. At the end of the day, the only person you can control is yourself. You are the model of success that others will learn from.

- Remember to trust your learners; they are your legacy.

- Articulate why you do this work. What is your moral imperative?

- If you want to change the educational landscape, you must first change yourself. You can't control others—only yourself.

- There is strength in numbers. The greater the unity of the movement, the better the chances of bringing our vision to life. Partner with people with different expertise than you; you will be better for it.

- Take your time getting everyone on board. Build a guiding coalition and move forward. Others will learn from your success.

- Keep your eye on the big picture. Don't get swallowed up by the details.

- Always speak the truth; this work is messy and initially hard to manage. Just be real about the failures, fits, and starts and celebrate success.

- Take risks, be patient, and don't give up.

- Accept feedback and input from others. Sustainable change takes a village.

- Envision success. What would your school be like if absolutely every student possessed learner agency? What will they think, say, and do when your Impact Team wildly succeeds?

# OUR INVITATION

We invite others to build on our thinking as we collectively advance efficacy, agency, and ownership for learners of all ages, regardless of their roles. Join our Leading Impact Team Facebook Group to collaborate with other innovative educators.

 **"We is smarter than me."**

# ONLINE
# APPENDIX

**Impact Teams Website**
*Templates, Forms,*
*Videos, Examples*

Case Studies

Impact Team
Facebook Group

Leading Impact Teams
Tips and Videos

Core Collaborative
YouTube Channel

# References and Further Reading

Ainsworth, L. (2011). *Rigorous curriculum design.* Lead + Learn Press.

Allen, K. A. (2023, June 27). Are we a part of nature or are we apart from nature?. Dr. Kathy Allen. https://kathleenallen.net/insights/are-we-a-part-of-nature-or-are-we-apart-from-nature/

Almarode, J. T., & Vandas, K. L. (2018). *Clarity for learning: Five essential practices that empower students and teachers.* Corwin.

Bandura, A. (1977). Self-efficacy: Toward a unifying theory of behavioral change. *Psychological Review, 84*(2), 191–215. https://doi.org/10.1037/0033-295X.84.2.191

Bandura, A. (1994). Self-efficacy. In V. S. Ramachaudran (Ed.), *Encyclopedia of human behavior* (Vol. 4, pp. 71–81). Academic Press.

Bandura, A. (1997). *Self-efficacy: The exercise of control.* W. H. Freeman and Company.

Bandura, A. (2000). *Exercise of human agency through collective efficacy.* Department of Psychology, Stanford University.

Barber, M. (2011). *Deliverology 101.* Corwin.

Barth, R. S. (2013). The time is ripe (again). *Educational Leadership, 71*(2), 15.

Baumeister, R., & Vohs, K. (2007). Self-regulation, ego depletion, and motivation. *Social and Personality Psychology Compass, 1*(1), 115–128.

Black, P., & Wiliam, D. (1998). Inside the black box: Raising standards through classroom assessment. *Phi Delta Kappan, 80*(2), 139–144, 146–148.

Bloomberg, P. J. (2012). *An examination of professional learning in two districts: Comparing the quality and quantity of network structure for improved achievement.* [Unpublished doctoral dissertation]. University of California San Diego. https://escholarship.org/uc/item/9nw3n332

Bloomberg, P. J., Vandas, K., Twyman, I., Dukes, V., Fairchild, R. C., Hamilton, C., & Wells, I. (2023). *Amplify learner voice through culturally responsive and sustaining assessment.* Mimi and Todd Press.

Bocala, C., & Boudett, K. P. (2022, February 1). Looking at data through an equity lens. *Educational Leadership, 79*(4). https://www.ascd.org/el/articles/looking-at-data-through-an-equity-lens

Bray, B., & McClaskey, K. (2017). *How to personalize learning: A guide for getting started and going deeper.* Corwin.

Brown, B. (2018). *Dare to lead: Brave work. Tough conversations. Whole hearts.*

Random House.

Brown, B. B. (2004). Adolescents' relationships with peers. In R. M. Lerner & L. Steinberg (Eds.), *Handbook of adolescent psychology* (pp. 363–394). John Wiley & Sons.

Brown, T. (2008). Design thinking. *Harvard Business Review, 92*(10), 86-93.

Bryk, A., & Schneider, B. (2003). Creating caring schools. *Educational Leadership, 60*(6), 40–45.

Bryk, A., & Schneider, B. (2022). *Core leadership principle: Relational trust.* School Leader Institute. https://education.nsw.gov.au/content/dam/main-education/en/home/school-leadership-institute/pllr-pdfs/Core_Leadership_Principle_Relational_Trust.pdf

California Department of Education. (2022). Asset-based pedagogies. https://www.cde.ca.gov/pd/ee/assetbasedpedagogies.asp

Calvert, L. (2016). The power of teacher agency: Why we must transform professional learning so that it really supports educator learning. *The Learning Professional: The Learning Forward Journal, 51*–56.

Clark, T. R. (2022, August 23). Don't let hierarchy stifle innovation. *Harvard Business Review.* https://hbr.org/2022/08/dont-let-hierarchy-stifle-innovation

Cobb, F., & Krownapple, J. (2019). *Belonging through a culture of dignity: The keys to successful implementation.* Mimi and Todd Press.

Coburn, C. E., Choi, L., & Mata, W. (2019). "I would go to her because her mind is math": Network formation in the context of a district-based mathematics reform. In A. J. Daly (Ed.), *Social network theory and educational change.* Harvard Education Press.

Covey, S. R., Covey, S., & Collins, J. (2020). *The 7 Habits of Highly Effective People 30th anniversary edition.* FranklinCovey Foundation.

Crooks, T. (1988). The impact of classroom evaluation practices on students. *Review of Educational Research, 58*(4), 438–481.

Curwin, R. L., & Mendler, A. N. (1988). *Discipline with dignity.* Association for Supervision and Curriculum Development.

Curwin, R. L., & Mendley, A. N. (1988). *Fair isn't equal: Seven classroom tips.* ASCD.

Daly, A., (Ed.), (2010). *Social Network Theory and Educational Change.* Cambridge, MA: Harvard Education Press.

DeMeester, K., & Jones, F. (2009). Formative assessment for PK–3 mathematics: A review of the literature. Retrieved from http://lsi.fsu.edu/Uploads/1/docs/Formative%20Assessment%20Lit%20Review%20OFCR-STEM.pdf

DeWitt, P. M. (2017). *Collaborative leadership: Six influences that matter most.* Corwin Press.

DeWitt, P. M. (2020). *Instructional leadership creating practice out of theory.* SAGE Publications.

Donohoo, J. (2017). *Collective efficacy: How educators' beliefs impact student learning.* Corwin.

Duke, N. K., & Pearson, P. (2002). *What research has to say about reading instruction* (3rd ed.). International Reading Association.

Dweck, C. (2006). *Mindset: The new psychology of success.* Ballantine Press.

Dweck, C. (2010). Mind-sets and equitable education. *Principal Leadership, 20*, 26–29.

Edmundson, A. (2012). *Teaming: How organizations learn, innovate, and compete in the knowledge economy.* Jossey-Bass.

Eells, R. (2011). *Meta-analysis of the relationship between collective teacher efficacy and student achievement.* UMI Publishing.

English, F. (2010). *Deciding what to teach and test: Developing, aligning and leading the curriculum.* Corwin.

Fencl, H., & Scheel, K. (2005). Research and teaching: Engaging students—an examination of the effects of teaching strategies on self-efficacy and course in a nonmajors physics course. *Journal of College Science Teaching, 35*(1), 20–24.

Finnigan, K., & Daly, A. (2013). System-wide reform in districts under pressure: The role of social networks in defining, acquiring, using, and diffusing research evidence. *Journal of Educational Administration, 51*(4), 476–497.

Fullan, M. (2002). Moral purpose writ large. *School Administrator, 59*(8), 14–16.

Fullan, M. (2010). *All systems go. The change imperative for whole system reform.* Corwin.

Fullan, M., & Quinn, J. (2016). *Coherence: The right divers in action for schools, districts, and systems.* Corwin.

Gallimore, R., Emerling, B., Saunders, W., & Goldenberg, C. (2009). Moving the learning of teaching closer to practice: Teacher education implications of school-based inquiry teams. *Elementary School Journal, The Chicago Press Journals, 109*(5), 537–553.

Gearhart & Osmundson (2009). Educational Assessment Vol.14, Iss. 1, (2009): 1-24.

Goddard, R. D., Hoy, W. K., & Hoy, A. W. (2000). Collective teacher efficacy: Its meaning, measure, and effect on student achievement. *American Education Research Journal, 37*(2), 479–507.

Goddard, R., Goddard, Y., Kim, E. S., & Miller, R. (2015). A theoretical and empirical analysis of the roles of instructional leadership, teacher collaboration, and collective efficacy beliefs in support of student learning. *American Journal of Education, 121*(4), 501–530. https://doi.org/10.1086/681925

González, N., Moll, L., & Amanti, C. (2005). *Funds of knowledge: Theorizing practices in households, communities, and classrooms.* Mahwah, NU: Routledge.

Graham, J. (2016, February 26). What Google learned from its quest to build the perfect team. *New York Times Magazine.* Retrieved from http://www.nytimes.com/2016/02/28/magazine/what-google-learned-from-its-quest-to-build-the-perfect-team.html?_r=0

Gregory, C., Cameron, C., & Davies, A. (2011). *Self-assessment and goal setting.* Solution Tree.

Gruenert, S., & Whitaker, T. (2015). *School culture rewired: How to define, assess, and transform it.* ASCD.

Hargreaves, A., & Fullan, M. (2012). *Professional capital: Transforming teaching in every school.* Teachers College Press.

Harvey, J., & Holland, H. (2012). *The school principal as leader: Guiding schools to bet-*

*ter teaching and learning*. The Wallace Foundation. Retrieved from http://bit.ly/zcvOCB

Hattie, J. (2015). High-impact leadership. *Educational Leadership, 72*(5), 36–40. Retrieved from http://bit.ly/17HMIk8

Hattie, J. A. (2009). *Visible learning: A synthesis of over 800 meta-analyses relating to achievement*. Routledge.

Hattie, J. A. (2012). *Visible learning for teachers: Maximizing impact on teachers*. Routledge.

Hattie, J. A. (2014, July). Keynote address. American Visible Learning Conference. Corwin.

Hattie, J. A. (2015a). *What doesn't work in education: The politics of distraction*. Pearson.

Hattie, J. A. (2015b). *What works in education: The politics of collaborative expertise*. Pearson.

Hattie, J. (2023). *Global research database*. Corwin Visible Learning Metax. Retrieved June 30, 2023, from https://www.visiblelearningmetax.com/Influences

Heritage, M. (2008). *Learning progressions: Supporting instruction and formative assessment*. Council of Chief State School Officers.

Heritage, M., Kim, J., Vendlinski, T. P., & Herman, J. (2009). From evidence to action: A seamless process in formative assessment? *Educational Measurement: Issues and Practice, 28*(3), 24–31.

Hoy, A. W. (2000). *Changes in teacher efficacy during the early years of teaching*. Paper presented at the Annual Meeting of the American Educational Research Association, New Orleans.

Hoy, W. K., & Sweetland, S. R., & Smith, P. (2002). Toward an organizational model of achievement in high schools: The significance of collective efficacy [Electronic version]. *Educational Administration Quarterly, 38*(1), 77–93.

Ingram, D., Louis, K. S., & Schroder, R. G. (2004). Accountability policies and teacher decision making: Barriers to the Use of Data to Improve Practice. *Teachers College Record, 106*(6), 1258-1287.

Jerald, C. D. (2007). *Believing and achieving* (Issue Brief). Center for Comprehensive School Reform and Improvement.

Knight, J., & Cornett, J. (n.d.). *Studying the impact on instructional coaching*. University of Kansas, Kansas Coaching Project at the Center of Research on Learning, and Department of Special Education.

Kotter, Inc. (2022). *8 steps to accelerate change in your organization*. https://www.kotterinc.com/8-steps-e-book-download/

Kotter, J. P. (1996). *Leading Change*. Boston: Harvard Business School Press.

Lawrence-Lightfoot, S., & Davis, J.J. (1997). *The art of science of portraiture*. San Francisco: Jossey-Bass.

Leana, C. R. (2011). The missing link in school reform. *Stanford Social Innovation Review*, Fall, 29–35.

Learning Forward. (2011). *Standards for professional learning*. https://standards.learningforward.org/

Margolis, H., & McCabe, P. (2006). Improving self-efficacy and motivation: What to do, what to say. *Intervention in School and Clinic, 41*(4), 218–227.

Marsh , E. (2019, July 9). The psychology of connected leadership. *T-Three.* August 28, 2023,

Marzano, R. J. (2003). *What works in schools: Translating research into action.* ASCD.

Marzano, R. J. (2012). *Marzano levels of school effectiveness.* Marzano Research Laboratory. https://www.wyoleg.gov/interimcommittee/2012/z02marzanolevels.pdf

Marzano, R. J., Kendall, J. S., & Gaddy, B. B. (1999). What should students know? Local control and the debate over essential knowledge. *American School Board Journal, 186*(9), 47–48, 66–62.

McDowell, M. (2018). *The lead learner: Improving clarity, coherence, and capacity for all.* Corwin.

Mer, B (December 17, 2020). "The Culture of White Supremacy in Organizations" Race, Research & Policy Portal. https://rrapp.hks.harvard.edu/the-culture-of-white-supremacy-in-organizations/

Meyer, D. K., Turner, J. C., & Spencer, C. A. (1997). Challenge in a mathematics classroom: Students' motivation and strategies in project-based learning. *Elementary School Journal, 97*(5), 501–521.

Milner, H. R. (2020). *Start where you are, but don't stay there: Understanding diversity, opportunity gaps, and teaching in today's classrooms.* Harvard Education Press.

Miskel, C., McDonald, D., & Bloom, S. (1983). Structural and expectancy linkages within schools and organizational effectiveness. *Educational Administration Quarterly, 19,* 49–82.

Mohr, B. J., & Watkins, J. M. (2002). *The essentials of appreciative inquiry: A roadmap for creating positive futures.* Pegasus Communications.

Moolenaar, N. M., Sleegers, P. J. C., & Daly, A. J. (2011). Ties with potential: Social network structure and innovative climate in Dutch schools. *Teachers College Record, 113*(9), 1983–2017.

Muhammad, G. E. (2020). *Cultivating genius: An equity framework for culturally and historically responsive literacy.* Scholastic.

Nelson, S. W., & Guerra, P. L. (2014). Educator beliefs and cultural knowledge: Implications for school improvement efforts. *Educational Administrative Quarterly, 50*(1), 67–95.

Nicol, D., & Macfarlane-Dick, D. (2005). *Formative assessment and self-regulated learning: A model and seven principles of good feedback practice.* Quality Assurance Agency for Higher Education.

O'Connell, M., & Vandas, K. (2015). *Partnering with students: Building ownership of learning.* Corwin.

OECD. (2008). Ten steps to equity in education. Retrieved from http://www.oecd.org/publications/Policybriefs

Schunk, D. H., & Pajares, F. (2002). The development of academic self-efficacy. In A. Wigfield & J. S. Eccles (Eds.), Development of achievement motivation (pp. 15-31).

Perkins, D. (2003). *King Arthur's round table: How collaborative conversations create smart organizations.* John Wiley & Sons.

Perkins, D. N., & Salomon, G. (1992). *Transfer of learning. Contribution to the International Encyclopedia of Education* (2nd ed.). Pergamon Press.

Peters, T. J., & Waterman, R. H. (1982). In search of excellence: Lessons from American's best run companies. Harper & Row.

Reeves, D. (2010). *Transforming professional development into student results.* ASCD.

Rerucha, M. Q. (2021). *Beyond the surface of restorative practices: Building a culture of equity, connection, and healing.* Dave Burgess Consulting.

Restorative Justice Consortium. (2004, December). *Principles of restorative processes* [rev. ed.]. Retrieved from https://www.iirp.edu/images/pdf/beth06_davey9.pdf

Richards, H., Brown, A., & Forde, T. (2007). Addressing diversity in schools: Culturally responsive pedagogy. *Teaching Exceptional Children, 39*(3), 64–68.

Robinson, V. M. J, Lloyd, C., Rowe, K. J. (2008). *The impact of leadership on student outcomes: An analysis of the different effects of leadership type.*

Rolheiser, C., & Ross, J. (2000). Student self-evaluation—What do we know? *Orbit, 30*(4), 33–36.

Ronfeldt, M., Farmer, S., McQueen, K., & Grissom, J. (2015). Teacher collaboration in instructional teams and student achievement. *American Educational Research Journal, 52*(3), 475–514.

Ross, J. A. (2006). The reliability, validity, and utility of self-assessment. *Practical Assessment Research & Evaluation, 11*(10), 1–13.

Safir, S., & Dugan, J. (2021). *Street data: A next-generation model for equity, pedagogy, and School Transformation.* SAGE PUBLICATIONS INC.

Schunk, D. H., & Pajares, F. (2002). *The development of academic self-efficacy.* In A. Wigfield & J. Eccles (Eds.), *Development of achievement motivation.* Academic Press.

Kim, S. (2008, December). The art of puzzles. TED Talk. https://www.ted.com/talks/scott_kim_the_art_of_puzzles?language=en

Senge, P. (1990). *The fifth discipline: The art and practice of the learning organization.* Doubleday.

Shafer, L. (2016). *Teaching together for change. Five factors that make teacher teams successful—and make schools stronger.* Retrieved from https://www.gse.harvard.edu/news/uk/16/02/teaching-together-change

Shepard, L. (2006). Classroom assessment. In R. L. Brennan (Ed.), *Educational measurement* (4th ed., pp. 623–646). Praeger.

Siciliano, M. (2016). It's the quality not the quantity of ties that matters: Social networks and self-efficacy beliefs. *American Education Research Journal, 53*(2), 227–262.

Stiggins, R. (2005). From formative assessment to assessment FOR learning: A path to success in standards-based schools. *Phi Delta Kappan, 87*(4), 324–328.

Stiggins, R. (2007). Assessment through the student's eyes. *Educating the Whole Child, 64*(8), 22–26.

Stiggins, R., & Chappuis, J. (2006). What a difference a word makes. *Journal of Staff Development, 27*(1).

Tschannen-Moran, M., Hoy, A. W., Hoy, & W. K. (1998). Teacher efficacy: Its meaning and measure. *Review of Educational Research, 68*(2), 202–248.

Tschannen-Moran, W. K., & Hoy, M. (2003). *Faculty survey, 2003*. Retrieved from http://mxtsch.people.wm.edu/ResearchTools/Faculty%20Trust%20Survey.pdf

Waters, S., Cross, D., & Shaw, T. (2010). Does the nature of schools matter? An exploration of selected school ecology factors on adolescent perceptions of school connectedness. *British Journal of Educational Psychology, 80*(3), 381–402. https://doi.org/10.1348/000709909X484479

Wilhelm, T. (2013). How principals cultivate shared leadership. *Educational Leadership, 71*(2), 62.

Wiliam, D. (2006). Formative assessment: Getting the focus right. *Educational Assessment, 11*, 283–289.

Woolfolk, A., & Shaughnessy, M. F. (2004). An interview with Anita Woolfolk: The educational psychology of teacher efficacy. *Educational Psychology Review, 16*(2), 153–176. http://www.jstor.org/stable/23363838

# Index

# Thank you!

Mimi & Todd Press exclusively publishes authors who are dedicated to making an impact through their work. By purchasing, reading and implementing their ideas, you deepen the impact and increase awareness for future learning.

## More from Mimi & Todd Press:

**Belonging Through a Culture of Dignity: The Keys to Successful Equity Implementation**

Floyd Cobb and John Krownapple

**The Project Habit: Making Rigorous PBL Doable**

Michael McDowell and Kelley S. Miller

**Amplify Learner Voice through Culturally Responsive and Sustaining Assessment**

Paul J. Bloomberg, Kara Vandas, Ingrid Twyman, et al.

**Learner Agency: A Field Guide for Taking Flight**

Kara Vandas, Jeanette Westfall, and Ashley Duvall

**Arrows: A Systems-Based Approach to School Leadership**

Carrie Rosebrock and Sarah Henry

**Peer Power: Unite, Learn and Prosper: Activate an Assessment Revolution**

Paul J. Bloomberg, Barb Pitchford, Kara Vandas, et al.

MIMI & TODD
—— PRESS ——
mimitoddpress.com

Mimi & Todd Press discovers and publishes purpose-driven thought leaders who are striving to make a difference in the world. Visit us online to browse our catalogue of books and learn more.